MW01155616

SPANISH GRAMMAR GUIDE FOR BEGINNERS

THE EXTENSIVE AND EASY STEP-BY-STEP APPROACH TO LEARNING SPANISH GRAMMAR

TEXTBOOK AND WORKBOOK

ISABEL NAVARRO TORRES – DANI RANGEL NIETO - JULIE HELLIWELL

CONTENTS

We wish to give special thanks to Dani Rangel Nieto for her outstanding dedication and commitment to writing this thorough and comprehensive guide to Spanish grammar. We also want to acknowledge Julie Helliwell for her valuable input and collaboration during the developmental stages and for editing and proofreading the book.

INTRODUCTION

Spanish Grammar Guide for Beginners is a complete, fully-comprehensive grammar guide and workbook aimed at people who have already started learning Spanish, but are within the beginner/elementary level (A1-A2) and have a genuine desire to engage in more in-depth studies to assimilate this beautiful language. It is also extremely beneficial for intermediate Spanish students (B1-B2) who want to consolidate previous learning and fill in any grammar gaps. When learning to speak a foreign language competently and positively, it is essential to start with a good, broad foundation, including grammar. But, contrary to popular opinion, learning grammar doesn't have to be boring: far from it!

First of all, let us assure you that the Spanish language is not complicated nor convoluted. It does not present any more significant complexities than the ones you face when learning any language other than your mother tongue. Spanish naturally has rules, norms, and parameters, but our all-encompassing studying and learning method will work wonderfully for you.

This extensive language guide and workbook has been made with dedication and affection, and we hope it will serve as an invaluable initial guide to your learning journey. It is divided into 22 chapters covering a broad spectrum of topics containing the essential vocabulary necessary when starting Spanish. In these chapters, you will find everything from greetings and courtesy rules; to the days of the week and months, the time, colors, food, and the climate. Plus, you will develop a strong foundation of Spanish grammar by reviewing verbs, adjectives, and pronouns, among other interesting and useful topics, so you can communicate with any Spanish speaker. It is written in workbook format with space to write your answers to all of the exercises.

Every chapter begins with a comprehensive explanation of the topic and vocabulary to be covered, including grammar rules and tips about Spanish speakers' customs. Chapters also include practical examples of all new vocabulary, paying particular attention to their common use. Although the book presents a general overview of the Spanish language that can be used in any circumstances, you may occasionally notice that the emphasis is on travelers, tourists, and those coming into contact with Hispanic culture for the first time.

A fundamental element of the workbook format is the abundance of practical exercises that accompany each of the 22 chapters. They are formulated as self-assessments, so you can immediately put into practice what you have learned about the topic you have just studied. These exercises are designed in a didactic and entertaining way to promote the ability to use the language. They are done in a simple but functional manner and will allow you to self-evaluate the level you have achieved. You will also find a translation exercise in each chapter to complete your holistic training and learning of this beautiful language. It is in the form of a series of frequently used, common, everyday phrases for you to translate from Spanish into English. Finally, we include short stories in every chapter that contain additional vocabulary and a few questions to check your comprehension of what you have just read. All the answers are at the end of each chapter, so you can analyze your results before revising any mistakes you have made or moving on to the next topic.

In today's globalized world, where borders are no longer represented in terms of distances or topographic spaces, we can access any geographic location through the click of a computer mouse and interact with people all over the world. Therefore, learning a foreign language in addition to our native tongue becomes a fundamental need for integral human development.

Every day, it is more and more evident that to understand, and possibly even to survive in the world that surrounds us, we need skills that perhaps weren't required by our parents. Not only is the use of technology essential today, so is the command of languages. From a technological, social, economic, educational, and humanistic perspective, the world's most powerful countries typically boast mastery of more than one language across their high school students, their young professionals, and their new generations.

By taking this book into your hands, you have already taken the first step, which is usually the most difficult: the decision to learn something new, no matter how old you are or your educational level or professional path. If you have already taken the initiative to learn a language other than your native one, you certainly deserve recognition and the word *¡Felicitaciones!*

The team that prepared this book would like to invite you to join us as we embark on a journey along the path to the Spanish language. The Spanish language is rich in history, origin, literary representatives, musicians, and poets. It is also rich in expressions and idioms that can have different meanings, depending on the country or region. But above all, it is rich in emotions because Spanish is a romantic, lyrical, and harmonious language to speak, write and listen to.

Now, without any further delay, go ahead and get started! We hope you find it useful and, above all, we we enjoy the book as much as we enjoyed writing it for you. It is our wish that this will be the first step on your route to mastering Spanish, so the only thing left for us to say is:

¡Bienvenido!

Chapter 1
GREETINGS

The first thing we should do when we arrive somewhere, meet someone new, or see an old acquaintance is to say hello. The first impression we make is important and says a lot about our upbringing and good behavior. In this chapter we will learn greetings and farewells in Spanish, how to introduce ourselves correctly, and how to start a conversation.

You should know that in Spanish there is an informal way and a formal way for almost all greetings and goodbyes. Informally we use the term **Tú** to refer to the other person, and the formal way is **Usted** which you can write with the abbreviation **Ud.**

Greetings:

- Informal greeting (suitable at any time of the day): Hola. - Hi.
- In the morning (before 12pm): Buenos días. - Good morning.
- In the afternoon (12pm to 7pm): Buenas tardes. - Good afternoon.
- At night (7pm until dawn): Buenas noches. - Good night.
- Informal: ¿Cómo estás? o ¿Cómo estás tú? - How are you?
- Formal: ¿Cómo está? o ¿Cómo está usted? - How are you?
- ¿Cómo has estado? - How have you been?
- ¿Cómo te va? - How are you doing?
- ¿Qué hay de nuevo? - What's new?
- Que gusto de verte. - Nice to see you.
- Tanto tiempo sin verte. - Long time no see.

Common responses when someone asks *"How are you?"*:

- Estoy bien. – I'm fine.
- Estoy muy bien. – I'm really well.

- Todo bien. – Everything's good.
- Estoy más o menos. – I'm ok. (average)
- Estoy mal. – I'm not well.

Introductions:

- Informal: Mucho gusto en concerte. - Nice to meet you.
- Formal: Mucho gusto en conocerlo. - Nice to meet you.
- Es un placer conocerlo. - It's a pleasure to meet you.
- Mucho gusto, mi nombre es… - Nice to meet you, my name is…
- ¿Cuál es tu nombre? - What is your name?
- Encantado de conocerlo. - Delighted to meet you.
- Hola, yo me llamo… - Hello, my name is…

Examples:

1. José: ¡Hola! Mucho gusto, mi nombre es José.

   Isabel: Encantada de conocerlo, yo me llamo Isabel.

   José: Hi! Nice to meet you, my name is José.

   Isabel: Delighted to meet you, my name is Isabel.

2. Pedro: Mi nombre es Pedro, ¿cómo te llamas?

   Ana: Mucho gusto, yo me llamo Ana.

   Pedro: El gusto es mío.

   Pedro: My name is Pedro, what is your name?

   Ana: Nice to meet you, my name is Ana.

   Pedro: The pleasure is mine.

3. Antonio: Hola ¿cómo te va?

   Ramón: Hola, bien, ¿y tú? ¿Cómo has estado?

   Antonio: Todo bien, gracias.

11

Antonio: Hi, how are you doing?

Ramon: Hello, good and you, how have you been?

Antonio: All good, thank you.

Farewells:

- Adiós. - Goodbye.

- Hasta luego. - See you later.

- Hasta mañana. - See you tomorrow.

- Nos vemos - See you.

- Hasta pronto - See you soon.

- Fue un placer conocerte. (Después de una presentación)
  - It was nice meeting you. (After an introduction)

- Hasta la próxima. - Until next time.

- Que te vaya bien. - Good luck to you.

- Te deseo lo mejor. - I wish you the best.

- Cuídate. - Take care.

- Chao. - Bye.

Examples:

1. Daniela: Adiós Marcos.

   Marcos: Adiós, hasta pronto.

   Daniela: Gracias, igual para ti.

   Daniela: Goodbye Marcos.

   Marcos: Bye, see you soon.

   Daniela: Thank you, the same to you.

2. Judith: Hasta luego, fue un placer conocerte.

   Juan: Igualmente, nos vemos mañana.

   Judith: See you later, it was nice meeting you.

Juan: Likewise, see you tomorrow.

3. Adriana: Chao.

    Carmen: Cuídate mucho.

    Adriana: Bye.

    Carmen: Take care.

———————————

Exercises:

1.- Write the appropriate greetings:

       1.1.- A las 9 de la noche: _____ _____

       1.2.- Informal: ¿Cómo _____?

       1.3.- A las 8 de la mañana: _____ _____

       1.4.- Informal (para cualquier hora del día): _____

       1.5.- A las 3 de la tarde: _____ _____

       1.6.- Formal: ¿Cómo _____?

       1.7.- A las 17:30: _____ _____

       1.8.- A las 11:00: _____ _____

       1.9.- A las 19:45: _____ _____

       1.10.- Formal: ¿Cómo _____ _____?

2. Complete the following brief conversations using your own information, paying attention to the formality of what is said.

       2.1.- Hola ¿Cuál es tu nombre?

          Tú: _____

       2.2.- Mucho gusto, mi nombre es Andrés.

          Tú: _____

       2.3.- Hola ¿Cómo te va?

          Tú: _____

       2.4.- Encantado de conocerlo, mi nombre es Daniel.

          Tú: _____

       2.5.- Hasta mañana.

          Tú: _____

       2.6.- Mi nombre es Carlos, mucho gusto.

          Tú: _____

       2.7.- Hasta luego, encantado de conocerte.

Tú: _____

2.8.- ¿Cómo está usted?

Tú: _____

 2.9.- Hola ¿Cómo estás tú?

Tú: _____

2.10.- ¿Cómo has estado?

Tú: _____

3.- Choose the form of response that you consider most appropriate from the three options that are given.

3.1.- Hola ¿Cómo estás tú?

a) Chao.

b) Bien, ¿y tú?

c) Hasta pronto.

3.2.- Mucho gusto, mi nombre es Nicolás.

a) Hasta mañana.

b) Bien, gracias.

c) Encantada, mi nombre es Daniela.

3.3.- Hola ¿cuál es tu nombre?

a) Hola, mi nombre es María.

b) Buenas noches.

c) Hasta luego.

3.4.- Adiós, nos vemos mañana.

a) Bien ¿y tú?

b) Hola, mi nombre es Juan.

c) Adiós, hasta mañana.

3.5.- Mucho gusto en conocerla.

a) Bien ¿y usted?

b) Encantado de conocerlo.

c) Hola.

3.6.- ¡Chao!

a) ¡Adiós!

b) ¡Hola!

c) ¿Cómo te va?

3.7.- ¿Cómo estás tú?

a) ¡Cuídate!

b) Bien, ¿y usted?

c) Bien, ¿y tú?

3.8.- ¿Cómo está usted?

a) ¡Chao!

b) Bien, ¿y tú?

c) Bien, ¿y usted?

3.9.- Hasta luego.

a) Hasta mañana.

b) ¿Qué me cuentas?

c) Hola.

3.10.- Adiós.

a) Hola.

b) ¿Cómo está?

c) Hasta luego.

4.- Select the appropriate answer from the column on the right.

4.1.- Saludo informal para cualquier hora.   A.- Fue un placer conocerte.

4.2.- ¿Cómo estás tú?   B.- Buenas tardes.

4.3.- ¿Cuál es tú nombre?   C.- Encantada, me llamo Ana.

4.4.- Saludo a las 9 de la mañana.   D.- Hola.

4.5.- Encantado de conocerte.   E.- Bien, gracias ¿y usted?

4.6.- Mucho gusto, mi nombre es Luís.   F.- Hasta pronto.

4.7.- Saludo a las 15:00.   G.- Bien, gracias ¿y tú?

4.8.- ¿Cómo está usted?   H.- Buenas noches.

4.9.- Saludo a las 20:30.   I.- Buenos días.

4.10.- Hasta luego.   J.- Mi nombre es Judith.

5.- Complete the following sentences:

5.1.- Hola mi amigo, ¿cómo _____?

5.2.- Buenas_____ (8pm)

5.3.- Víctor: Hasta mañana Ana, mucho gusto en conocerla.

    Ana: Hasta mañana, Fue _____ Víctor.

5.4.- Adriana: Hola ¿Cuál es tú nombre?

    Carlos: Hola. Mi _____.

5.5.- Buenas _____ (4:30pm)

5.6.- ¿Cómo te va?

    _____, gracias.

5.7.- Judith: Mucho gusto, mi nombre es Judith.

    Manuel:_____ mi _____ es Manuel.

5.8.- Buenos _____ (10am)

5.9.- ¿Cómo está usted?

    _____, gracias ¿y _____?

5.10.- ¿Cómo estás tú?

    _____, gracias, ¿y _____?

Translations:

Translate the following sentences into English:

     1.- ¡Hola! ¿Cómo te va?

     2.- Buenos días, es una hermosa mañana.

     3.- Hasta mañana, fue un placer conocerte.

     4.- ¿Cómo estás? Tanto tiempo sin verte.

     5.- Mi nombre es Daniel, ¿Cuál es tu nombre?

     6.- Buenas noches, nos vemos mañana.

     7.- Hasta luego, cuídate.

     8.- Mucho gusto, mi nombre es Ismael.

     9.- Buenas tardes, vamos a tomarnos un café.

     10.- ¡Chao! ¡Cuídate mucho! Nos vemos mañana.

Story:

Es una **hermosa mañana** en el **vecindario**, y dos **mujeres** salen de sus **casas** y se encuentran por primera vez. "Hola," le dice Teresa a su **nueva vecina**, "Es un placer conocerla." La otra mujer **sonríe**. "Buenos días," y le ofrece una mano a Teresa, "Mucho gusto, mi nombre es Caterina. ¿Cuál es tu **nombre**?" Teresa también **sonríe** y responde: "Yo me llamo Teresa, soy tu **nueva vecina**." Caterina le pregunta: "¿Cómo te va? ¿Te gusta tu **casa**?" Y Teresa **sonríe**, "Estoy bien. Amo mi **casa nueva**." Caterina le da un **abrazo** a Teresa y se despiden. "Fue un placer conocerte," dice Teresa. Y Caterina le responde "Hasta la próxima."

Después de un año, Teresa y Caterina son amigas. En la **mañana** se saludan con un **abrazo**. "¡Hola!" dice Teresa, "¿Cómo estás?" Caterina le responde: "Estoy muy bien. ¿Qué hay de nuevo?" Teresa **sonríe** y le dice, "Nada nuevo. ¿Quieres almorzar juntas?" Caterina acepta. "Si, me encantaría," dice y luego se despide, "Hasta luego." "Chao," dice Teresa con otro **abrazo**.

Vocabulary List:

1. Hermosa – Beautiful
2. Mañana – Morning
3. Vecindario – Neighborhood
4. Mujeres – Women
5. Casa – House

6. Nueva – New
7. Vecina – Neighbor
8. Sonríe – Smiled
9. Nombre – Name
10. Abrazo – Hug

Translated Story:

It is a **beautiful morning** in the **neighborhood**, and two **women** leave their houses and meet for the first time. "Hello," Teresa says to her **new neighbor**, "It's a pleasure to meet you." The other woman **smiled.** "Good morning", and she offered her hand to Teresa, "Pleased to meet you, my name is Caterina. What is your **name**?" Teresa also **smiled** and responded, "My name is Teresa, I'm your **new neighbor**." Caterina asked her, "How are you doing? Do you like your new **house**?" And Teresa **smiled**, "I'm fine. I love my **new house**". Caterina gives Teresa a **hug** and they say goodbye. "It was nice meeting you," says Teresa. And Caterina responds, "Until next time."

A year later, Teresa and Caterina are friends. In the **morning** they greet each other with a **hug**. "Hello!" says Teresa, "How are you?" Caterina responds, "I'm very well. What's new?" Teresa **smiled** and says to her, "Nothing new. Do you want to have lunch together?" Caterina accepts. "Yes, I'd love to," she says and then she says goodbye, "See you later." "Bye," says Teresa with another **hug**.

Questions:

1. ¿La historia se desarrolla en la mañana, tarde, o noche? _____
   Does the story develop in the morning, afternoon or evening?

2. ¿Cuántas personas estaban hablando? _____
   How many people were talking?

3. ¿Eran hombres o mujeres? _____
   Were they men or women?

4. ¿Cómo se llamaban las mujeres? _____
   What were the women called?

5. ¿De dónde salieron las mujeres? _____
   Where did the women come out of?

6. ¿Cuánto tiempo pasó para que se hicieran amigas? _____
   How much time passed before they became friends?

Answers:

1.1.- Buenas noches

1.2.- estás

1.3.- Buenos días

1.4.- Hola

1.5.- Buenas tardes

1.6.- está

1.7.- Buenas tardes

1.8.- Buenos días

1.9.- Buenas noches

1.10.- está usted

2.1.- Hola, mi nombre es (tu nombre).

2.2.- Encantado (o mucho gusto en conocerlo) yo me llamo (tu nombre).

2.3.- Hola, bien gracias.

2.4.- Mucho gusto (o es un placer conocerlo) mi nombre es (tú nombre).

2.5.- Hasta mañana.

2.6.- Encantado (o un placer) mi nombre es (tú nombre).

2.7.- Adiós (o hasta pronto o hasta luego) fue un placer conocerte.

2.8.- Bien, gracias ¿y usted?

2.9.- Hola bien, gracias ¿y tú?

2.10.- Bien, gracias.

3.1.- b

3.2.- c

3.3.- a

3.4.- c

3.5.- b

3.6.- a

3.7.- c

3.8.- c

3.9.- a

3.10.- c

4.1.- D

4.2.- G

4.3.- J

4.4.- I

4.5.- A

4.6.- C

4.7.- B

4.8.- E

4.9.- H

4.10.- F

5.1.- estás

5.2.- noches

5.3.- un placer conocerlo

5.4.- nombre es Carlos

5.5.- tardes

5.6.-Bien

5.7.- Encantado (o un placer, o mucho gusto) / nombre

5.8.- días

5.9.- Bien / usted?

5.10.- Bien / tú?

Translations:

1.- Hello! How are you doing?

2.- Good morning, it is a beautiful morning.

3.- See you tomorrow, it was a pleasure meeting you.

4.- How are you? Long time no see.

5.- My name is Daniel, what is your name?

6.- Good night, see you tomorrow.

7.- See you later, take care.

8.- Nice to meet you, my name is Ismael.

9.- Good afternoon, let's have a coffee.

10.- Bye! Take care! See you tomorrow.

Story:

1. Mañana. – Morning.

2. Dos. – Two.

3. Mujeres – Women.

4. Teresa y Caterina. – Teresa and Caterina.

5. De sus casas. – From their houses.

6. Un año. – One year.

Chapter 2
COURTESY RULES

In any language, it is essential to know the rules of courtesy to be able to function socially in a correct way. So, after practicing greetings in Spanish, we are going to review some words that allow us to have a fluid conversation while showing respect to the person we're talking with.

There are universal norms of behavior such as being punctual, giving a seat to pregnant women and the elderly, looking at whoever is speaking to us, and chewing with your mouth closed, among many others. In this chapter, we are going to study words that compliment good behavior including the most frequently used, **please** and **thank you**, along with others that will highlight our educational and cultural level.

Thank you: Gracias

It is the expression that we use to give thanks for something or express gratitude.

Examples:

1. - Pase adelante.

   - Gracias.

   - Come on in.

   - Thank you.

2. - Gracias por haber venido.

   - Thank you for coming.

3. - Este es su asiento.

   - Muchas gracias.

   - This is your seat.

   - Thank you very much.

4. - Estoy muy agradecido por su ayuda.

   - I am very thankful for your help.

5. - Le agradezco que me permita pasar.

   - Thank you for allowing me to pass.

6. - ¿Desea tomar una copa?

   - No gracias.

   -Do you want a drink?

   - No thanks.

You're welcome and It's nothing: De nada and Por nada

These words are often used to respond to gratitude, after someone says "*thank you.*"

   Examples:

1. - Carlos: Puede sentarse aquí.

   - Ana: Gracias.

   - Carlos: De nada.

   - Carlos: You can sit here.

   - Ana: Thank you.

   - Carlos: You're welcome.

2. - Cliente: Camarero, me trae una soda por favor.

   - Camarero: Su soda caballero.

   - Cliente: Muchas gracias.

   - Camarero: De nada.

   - Customer: Waiter bring me a soda please.

   - Waiter: Your soda sir.

   - Client: Thank you very much.

   - Waiter: You're welcome.

26

3. - Gracias por esperarme.

    - Por nada.

    - Thanks for waiting for me.

    - It's nothing.

Please: Por Favor

It is always written as two separate words, and is used when we want to ask for something in a polite way.

Examples:

1. - ¿Me pasa la sal, por favor?

    - Could you pass me the salt please?

2. - Por favor me dice dónde queda la catedral.

    - Please tell me where the cathedral is.

3. - Me vende por favor un boleto.

    - Please sell me a ticket.

4. - Por favor me dice el precio del pan.

    - Pease tell me the price of bread.

5. - Les pido por favor que hagan silencio.

    - I ask you all to please be quiet.

6. - ¿Quiere un café?

    -Si, por favor.

    -Would you like a coffee?

    -Yes, please.

Sorry and Excuse me: Perdón and Disculpe

These are expressions that we can use to apologize or ask for forgiveness in everyday situations, for example if we accidentally bump into someone at the supermarket. In an interrogative way they are usually used to ask for something to be repeated which we did not understand or hear well. Also, they are used to request something in a respectful way.

Examples:

1. - Disculpe, me trae el menú.

    - Excuse me, bring me the menu.

2. - Perdón por la tardanza.

    - Sorry for the delay.

3. - ¿Perdón? No entendí lo que dijo.

    - Sorry? I didn't understand what he said.

4. - Disculpe, ¿me puede dar la hora?

    - Excuse me, can you tell me the time?

5. - Perdón, no fue mi intención pisarle el pie.

    - Sorry, I didn't mean to step on your foot.

6. - Disculpe que la interrumpa ¿puedo hacerle una pregunta?

    - Excuse me for interrupting, can I ask you a question?

Welcome: Bienvenido

This expression is used to receive or greet someone.

Examples:

1. - Bienvenida a mi casa.

   - Welcome to my house.

2. - Bienvenidos a la conferencia.

   - Welcome to the conference.

3. - Sean cordialmente bienvenidos a nuestras instalaciones.

   - You are cordially welcome to our facilities.

Excuse me: Con permiso

This is a different courtesy rule that is used to ask to be authorized to speak, enter or leave somewhere, also to do things like take a seat, occupy a place, move elsewhere, take something, and more.

Examples:

1. - Con permiso, me retiro.

   - If you'll excuse me, I'm leaving.

2. - Buenos días, con permiso ¿puedo pasar?

   - Good morning, excuse me, can I come in?

3. - Con permiso voy a colocar aquí mi vaso.

   - Excuse me, I am going to place my glass here.

4. - Con permiso diré unas palabras.

   - If you'll allow me, I'll say a few words.

———————————

Exercises:

1.- Complete the following conversations with the correct alternative from the options in brackets.

    1.1.- Buenas tardes, ¿me dice la hora ___ _____? (permiso, de nada, por favor)

    1.2.- - _____, ¿puedo pasar? (disculpe, adiós, bienvenido)

    1.3.- - ¿Me permite un bolígrafo?

       - Aquí tiene.

       - _____. (por favor, gracias, por nada)

    1.4.- - Gracias por traer mi equipaje.

       - _____ _____ (disculpe, hola, de nada)

    1.5.- ____ _____, voy a pasar. (hasta luego, con permiso, gracias)

    1.6.- _____ por llegar tarde. (por favor, de nada, perdón)

    1.7.- - Chofer: ¿A dónde la llevo?

       - Pasajera: Al aeropuerto __ _____ (de nada, bienvenido, por favor)

    1.8.- Pasen adelante y sean _____ a nuestra casa (gracias, bienvenidos, con permiso)

    1.9.- _____ ¿puede bajar el volumen? (disculpe, mucho gusto, por nada)

    1.10.- - Laura: ¿Qué hora es?

       - Simón: Las 3 y 45.

       - Laura: _____. (Chao, De nada, Gracias)

2.- Select the most appropriate response in each situation.

    2.1.- Gracias por prestarme su celular.

      a) Por favor.

      b) Bienvenida.

      c) De nada.

2.2.- Siéntese en mi puesto, si gusta.

   a) Gracias.

   b) Hasta luego.

   c) Disculpe.

2.3.- ¡Señor. Ud. me acaba de pisar!

   a) De nada.

   b) Perdón.

   c) Agradecido.

2.4.- ¿Desea un café?

   a) Sea bienvenido.

   b) Sí.

   c) Sí, gracias.

2.5.- Gracias por recibirnos en su casa.

   a) Por nada, bienvenidos.

   b) Con permiso.

   c) Hasta mañana.

2.6.- ¿Quiere algo de la cocina?

   a) Sí, una ensalada ¡rápido!

   b) Sí, una ensalada.

   c) Sí, una ensalada por favor.

2.7.- Si no hay más preguntas, me retiro.

   a) ¡No! ahora voy yo a preguntar.

   b) Disculpe, ¿me permite hacerle una última pregunta?

   c) Quiero hacer una pregunta.

2.8.- ¿Quiere otra copa?

    a) Sí, adiós.

    b) No quiero más.

    c) No, muchas gracias.

2.9.- ¿Llegaron bien al hotel?

    a) Sí, todos bien. Gracias por preguntar.

    b) Sí, llegamos.

    c) Sí, ya llegamos, adiós.

2.10.- Buenas noche Señor Moreno, sus boletos están en la recepción.

    a) Ok.

    b) Está bien.

    c) Muchas gracias, es Ud. muy amable.

3.- Complete the conversations from the two options given in brackets.

    3.1.- -¿Me dice la hora _____?

      - Son las 9 y 15.

      - _____.

    (gracias / por favor)

    3.2.- - _____, voy a entrar a su oficina.

      - Sí pase_____.

    (por favor / con permiso)

    3.3.- - Camarero, _____ ¿me trae otro tenedor?

      - Sí aquí tiene.

      - Muchas _____.

(gracias / por favor)

3.4.- - _____, creo que Ud. está sentado en mi puesto.

   - Es cierto. Ud. _____.

   (disculpe / perdóneme)

3.5.- - Buenas tardes. _____ ¿puedo sentarme aquí?

   - Sí, _____ siéntese.

   (por favor / con permiso)

3.6.- - _____ por ayudarme con mis maletas.

   - _____, fue un placer.

   (gracias / de nada)

3.7.- - Tome asiento, _____.

   - _____ por invitarme.

   (gracias / por favor)

3.8.- - _____ a la conferencia.

   - Muy _____ por su hospitalidad.

   (agradecido / bienvenido)

3.9.- - _____ por llegar tarde.

   - No se preocupe, pase _____.

   (por favor / disculpe)

3.10.- - _____ por prestarme su bolígrafo.

   - _____. Encantado de ayudarle.

   (por nada / gracias)

4.- Answer the following questions in Spanish, according to what you have studied in this chapter.

4.1.- Word used to welcome or receive someone.

_____

4.2.- How do we respond when someone says *Gracias*?

_____

4.3.- What words do we use if we want to ask something politely?

_____

4.4.- Word we use to give thanks for something.

_____

4.5.- What expression do we use if we bump into someone on the subway?

_____

4.6.- Words that we use to ask for permission when entering a place.

_____

4.7.- If someone says: *Tráeme un vaso de agua!* What courtesy formula is missing?

_____

4.8.- If someone does us a favor, how can we respond?

_____

4.9.- If we are late for a meeting, what word do we use to apologize?

_____

4.10.- If they tell us *Gracias*, we must respond with:

_____

5.- Select the correct answer from the column on the right.

5.1.- Estoy muy _____ por su respuesta.

A.- No, gracias

5.2.- Gracias por su ayuda.

B.- disculpan

5.3.- Sean _____ a la reunión anual.

C.- agradezco

5.4.- Me trae un refresco_____.

D.- Perdón

5.5.- Uds. me _____, yo me retiro.

E.- Disculpe

5.6.- _____ si lo pise.

F.- bienvenidos

5.7.- Le _____ su cooperación.

G.- agradecido

5.8.- _____ me repite, no lo escuché.

H.- Gracias

5.9.- ¿Desea otra copa de vino?

I.- por favor

5.10.- Aquí está su maleta.

J.- De nada

Translations:

Please translate the following sentences into English.

1.- **Por favor** me trae un vaso de agua.

_____

2.- Me siento muy **agradecido** por todas sus atenciones.

_____

3.- **Con permiso**, debo retirarme a mi habitación, buenas noches.

_____

4.- **Bienvenidos** todos, a la conferencia de prensa.

_____

5.- **Disculpen** las molestias ocasionadas.

_____

6.- **Gracias** a todos los que colaboraron con la recaudación.

_____

7.- **Por favor** dejar limpio todo antes de retirarse.

_____

8**.- De nada**. Fue un placer poder ayudarlos, **por favor** vuelvan pronto.

_____

9.- **Perdonen** la demora en la entrega de los resultados.

_____

10.- **Muchas gracias** por escucharnos.

_____

Story:

Ana tiene una **entrevista** de **trabajo** el día de hoy. Es un **trabajo** muy importante, así que ella se siente nerviosa. Ana se despertó muy **temprano**, pero tardó mucho **tiempo** escogiendo qué ropa ponerse, y ahora es un poco **tarde**. Antes de salir de su casa, Ana revisa el mensaje que recibió de la **oficina** el día anterior. "Buenas tardes. Muchas gracias por su interés en el puesto de **trabajo**. Por favor, pase por la **oficina** mañana a las 10 de la mañana."

En el camino de su casa a la **oficina**, Ana tuvo algunos problemas. Cuando casi choca con **alguien** por **caminar** muy **rápido**, Ana **dijo**: "¡Perdón! Se me hizo **tarde**." Cuando subió a un taxi, le pidió al conductor: "Disculpe, ¿podría ir más **rápido**?" Y cuando al fin llegó a la **entrevista**, lo primero que **dijo** fue: "Buenos días. Vengo a la **entrevista** de **trabajo**. Disculpen mi tardanza." Pero su futuro jefe le sonrió muy amablemente y le **dijo**, "¡Bienvenida! No se preocupe. En realidad, llega justo a **tiempo**. Por favor, tome asiento."

Vocabulary List:

1. Entrevista – Interview
2. Trabajo – Job
3. Temprano – Early
4. Tiempo – Time
5. Oficina – Office
6. Tarde – Late
7. Caminar – Walk
8. Rápido – Fast
9. Alguien – Someone
10. Dijo – Said

Translated Story:

Ana has a **job interview** today. It is a very important job, so she feels nervous. Ana woke up very early, but took a long **time** choosing what clothes to wear, and now she is running a little late. Before leaving the house, Ana revises the message that she received from the **office** the day before. "Good afternoon. Many thanks for your interest in the **job** position. Please come to the **office** tomorrow at 10am".

On the way from her house to the **office**, Ana had some problems. When she almost crashed into **someone** due to **walk**ing so **fast**, Ana **said**, "Sorry! I'm late." When she got in a taxi, she asked the driver, "Excuse me, could you go faster?" And when she finally arrived at the interview, the first thing that she **said** was, "Good morning. I have come for the **job** interview. Excuse my delay." But her future boss smiled at very nicely and **said**, "Welcome! Don't worry. Actually, you've arrived just on time. Please, sit down".

Questions:

1. ¿Ana se despertó temprano o tarde? _____
   Did Ana wake up early or late?

2. ¿A dónde iba Ana? _____
   Where was Ana going?

3. ¿A qué hora era la entrevista? _____
   What time was the interview?

4. ¿Ana caminaba rápido o lento? _____
   Was Ana walking fast or slow?

5. ¿Qué le pidió Ana al taxi? _____
   What did Ana ask the taxi to do?

6. ¿Quién le dio la bienvenida a Ana? _____
   Who welcomed Ana?

Answers:

1.1.- por favor?

1.2.- Disculpe

1.3.- Gracias

1.4.- De nada.

1.5.- con permiso

1.6.- Perdón

1.7.- por favor.

1.8.- bienvenidos

1.9.- Disculpe

1.10.- Gracias.

2.1.- c

2.2.- a

2.3.- b

2.4.- c

2.5.- a

2.6.- c

2.7.- b

2.8.- c

2.9.- a

2.10.- c

3.1.- -¿Me dice la hora por favor?

    - Son las 9 y 15.

    - Gracias.

3.2.- - Con permiso voy a entrar a su oficina.

    - Sí, pase, por favor.

3.3.- - Camarero. Por favor ¿me trae otro tenedor?

- Sí aquí tiene.

- Muchas gracias.

3.4.- - Disculpe, creo que Ud. está sentado en mi puesto.

- Es cierto. Ud. perdóneme.

3.5.- - Buenas tardes. Con permiso ¿puedo sentarme aquí?

- Sí por favor, siéntese.

3.6.- - Gracias por ayudarme con mis maletas.

- De nada, fue un placer.

3.7.- - Tome asiento por favor.

- Gracias por invitarme.

3.8.- - Bienvenido a la conferencia.

- Muy agradecido por su hospitalidad.

3.9.- - Disculpe por llegar tarde.

- No se preocupe, pase por favor.

3.10.- - Gracias por prestarme su bolígrafo.

- Por nada. Encantado de ayudarle.

4.1.- Bienvenido

4.2.- De nada o por nada

4.3.- Por favor

4.4.- Gracias

4.5.- Disculpe o perdón

4.6.- Con permiso

4.7.- Por favor

4.8.- Gracias, o Estoy muy agradecido por su ayuda.

4.9.- Disculpe o perdón

4.10.- Por nada o de nada

5.1.- G

5.2.- J

5.3.- F

5.4.- I

5.5.- B

5.6.- D

5.7.- C

5.8.- E

5.9.- A

5.10.- H

Translations:

1.- **Please** can you bring me a glass of water.

2.- I am very **thankful** for all your attention.

3.- **Excuse me,** I must retire to my room, good night.

4.- **Welcome,** everyone, to the press conference.

5.- **Sorry** for the inconvenience caused.

6.- **Thanks** to all who collaborated with the collection.

7.- **Please** leave everything clean before leaving.

8.**- You're welcome**. It was a pleasure to help you, **please** come back soon.

9.- **Forgive** the delay in delivering the results.

10.- **Thank you very much** for listening to us.

<u>Story</u>:

1. Temprano - early
2. A la oficina – to the office
3. A las 10 de la mañana – at 10am
4. Rápido - fast
5. Que fuera más rápido – to go faster
6. Su futuro jefe – her future boss

Chapter 3
NUMBERS

When we interact with people in another language, it is very useful to know the numbers correctly. This can help us to avoid many problems. For example, if we are trying to find an address, or when we want to know the cost of something, such as a ticket, a meal, the price of a hotel room etc.

In this chapter, we will introduce you to the numbers in Spanish, their pronunciation, how to write them, and the different ways you might see them.

Before practicing all the numbers, you should know that, in Spanish, there are two forms or categories of numbers:

Cardinal Numbers: used to count 1 (one), 2 (two), 3 (three)…

    Examples:

1. - Tengo cinco (5) hermanos.

   - I have five (5) siblings.

2. - Tengo veintidós (22) años.

   - I am twenty-two (22) years old.

3. - América fue descubierta en mil cuatrocientos noventa y dos. (1492)

   - America was discovered in fourteen ninety-two. (1492)

Ordinal Numbers: used to give sequence order 1st (first) 2nd (second) 3rd (third)...

    Examples:

1. - Brasil está de primero (1°) en la clasificación al mundial de fútbol.

   - Brazil is first (1st) in qualifying for the World Cup.

2. - Yo vivo en el noveno (9°) piso de ese edificio.

    - I live on the ninth (9th) floor of that building.

3. - Es la tercera (3°) vez que te lo digo.

    - It is the third (3rd) time I have told you.

Now that we have clarified this point, we are going to learn all the numbers in both forms. Let's start with the cardinals.

Cardinal numbers:

Of course, we'll start with the numbers from 0 to 9.

0 = cero

1 = uno / una / un

2 = dos

3 = tres

4 = cuatro

5 = cinco

6 = seis

7 = siete

8 = ocho

9 = nueve

Examples:

1. - Me gustaría tener dos (2) perritos.

    - I would like to have two (2) puppies.

2. - La niña ya tiene cuatro (4) dientes.

    - The girl already has four (4) teeth.

3. - Por favor quisiera siete (7) entradas para el concierto.

    - I would like seven (7) tickets to the concert please.

From 10 to 30, each number has its own name, which is a single word:

    10 = diez

    11 = once

    12 = doce

    13 = trece

    14 = catorce

    15 = quince

    16 = dieciséis

    17 = diecisiete

    18 = dieciocho

    19 = diecinueve

    20 = veinte

    21 = veintiuno

    22 = veintidós

    23 = veintitrés

    24 = veinticuatro

    25 = veinticinco

    26 = veintiséis

    27 = veintisiete

    28 = veintiocho

    29 = veintinueve

    30 = treinta

Examples:

1. - Ese libro cuesta veintitrés (23) euros.

   - That book costs twenty-three (23) euros.

2. - Mi hermano tiene dieciséis (16) años.

   - My brother is sixteen (16) years old.

3. - Era una pared de catorce (14) metros de largo.

   - It was a wall fourteen (14) meters long.

From 30 and onwards, the numbers are written with the tens and the units separately, linking them together with 'and' (*y*):

   31 = treinta y uno / una / un

   32 = treinta y dos

   33 = treinta y tres

And so on for all tens:

   40 = cuarenta

   41 = cuarenta y uno

   42 = cuarenta y dos

   50 = cincuenta

   51 = cincuenta y uno

   60 = sesenta

   61 = sesenta y uno

   70 = setenta

   80 = ochenta

   90 = noventa

   98 = noventa y ocho

   99 = noventa y nueve

Examples:

1. - Mi padre tiene cincuenta y dos (52) años.

    - My father is fifty-two (52) years old.

2. - En la hacienda mi abuelo tenía setenta y seis (76) vacas.

    - On the farm my grandfather had seventy-six (76) cows.

3. - El hospital tiene disponibles ochenta y cuatro (84) camas.

    - The hospital has eighty-four (84) beds available.

Hundreds:

The number 100 can be written in two different ways. It is written as **cien** when it is exactly 100, when it goes before a noun, or to say the numbers one hundred thousand and one hundred million.

Examples:

1. - Tengo cien historias que contarte.

    - I have a hundred stories to tell you.

2. - Cien autos en la autopista.

    - A hundred cars on the highway.

3. - Cien hermosas aves.

    - One hundred beautiful birds.

4. - Cien mil estrellas radiantes.

    - One hundred thousand radiant stars.

We write **ciento** when it is followed by another number, or is in the plural.

Examples:

1. - Eran ciento uno (101) los que lo acompañaron.

   - There were one hundred and one (101) who accompanied him.

2. - Son ciento dos (102) dólares la entrada.

   - It's one hundred and two (102) dollars a ticket.

3. - Vimos cientos de estrellas en el cielo.

   - We saw hundreds of stars in the sky.

   The rest of the hundreds are as follows:

   100 = cien / ciento

   101 = ciento uno

   102 = ciento dos

   199 = ciento noventa y nueve

   200 = doscientos

   201 = doscientos uno

   202 = doscientos dos

   300 = trescientos

   400 = cuatrocientos

   500 = quinientos

   600 = seiscientos

   700 = setecientos

   800 = ochocientos

   900 = novecientos

   998 = novecientos noventa y ocho

   999 = novecientos noventa y nueve

<u>Examples:</u>

1. - Murieron más de trescientos (300) hombres en batalla.

    - More than three hundred (300) men died in battle.

2. - Pudimos contar trescientas setenta y cinco (375) palabras.

    - We were able to count three hundred and seventy-five (375) words.

3. - Ya eran seiscientos ochenta y dos (682) los casos reportados.

    - There were already six hundred and eighty-two (682) reported cases.

1,000 to 1,000,000:

Now we will deal with two new words: **mil** (1,000) and **millón** (1,000,000). The comma that divides the thousands from hundreds in English is replaced with a full stop.

1000 = mil

1001 = mil uno

1100 = mil cien

1999 = mil novecientos noventa y nueve

2000 = dos mil

3000 = tres mil

10.000 = diez mil

20.000 = veinte mil

90.000 = noventa mil

100.000 = cien mil

200.000 = doscientos mil

300.000 = trescientos mil

400.000 = cuatrocientos mil

900.000 = novecientos mil

999.999 = novecientos noventa y nueve mil novecientos noventa y nueve

1.000.000 = un millón

Uno, una y un:

The numbers one and the twenty-one use are shortened when they go before a noun, adjective or another number and become **un** and **veintiún** respectively. They also have feminine alternatives, **una** and **veintiuna** if they precede feminine words.

Examples:

1. - Un (1) gato callejero.
    - One (1) stray cat.

2. - Un (1) bonito sombrero.
    - One (1) nice hat.

3. - Veintiún (21) días para mi cumpleaños.
    - Twenty-one (21) days to my birthday.

4. - Cincuenta y un (51) dólares.
    - Fifty-one (51) dollars.

5. - Una (1) manzana muy apetitosa.
    - One (1) very appetizing apple.

6. - Una (1) enorme casa.
    - One (1) huge house.

7. - Treinta y una (31) hojas tenía el documento.
    - The document had thirty-one (31) pages.

<u>Ordinal Numbers</u>:

At the beginning of the topic, we explained that these serve to give an order of sequence. The suffixes 'st', 'rd' and 'th' in English are replaced with a '°':

1° = primero

2° = segundo

3° = tercero

4° = cuarto

5° = quinto

6° = sexto

7° = séptimo

8° = octavo

9° = noveno

10° = décimo

11° = decimoprimero o undécimo

12° = decimosegundo o duodécimo

13° = decimotercero

14° = decimocuarto

15° = decimoquinto

16° = decimosexto

17° = decimoséptimo

18° = decimoctavo

19° = decimonoveno

20° = vigésimo

21° = vigesimoprimero

22° = vigesimosegundo

30° = trigésimo

31° = trigésimo primero

32° = trigésimo segundo

40° = cuadragésimo

50° = quincuagésimo

60° = sexagésimo

70° = septuagésimo

80° = octogésimo

90° = nonagésimo

99° = nonagésimo noveno

100° = centésimo

1.000° = milésimo

1.000.000° = millonésimo

Examples:

1. - El sospechoso vive en el decimocuarto (14°) piso.

    - The suspect lives on the fourteenth (14th) floor.

2. - Ella es mi primer (1°) y único amor.

    - She is my first (1st) and only love.

3. - Bienvenidos a nuestra fiesta del vigesimosexto (26°) aniversario.

    - Welcome to our twenty-sixth (26th) anniversary party.

Gender, number and when to shorten:

Unlike cardinal numbers, ordinals must agree in gender with the noun that accompanies it. Plural forms end as usual with the letter **s**.

Examples:

1. - Era la tercera (3°) maestra que tenían.

    - She was the third (3rd) teacher that they had.

2. - Me tocó tomar el cuarto (4°) autobús.

   - I had to take the fourth (4th) bus.

3. - Ana y Elisa fueron las primeras (1°) en llegar al evento.

   - Ana and Elisa were the first (1st) to arrive at the event.

However, the ordinal numbers **primero (1st)** and **tercero (3rd)** are shortened to **primer** and **tercer** respectively when accompanied by a singular masculine noun.

Examples:

1. - Arturo era su tercer (3°) esposo.

   - Arturo was her third (3rd) husband.

2. - Julia llegará en el primer (1°) vuelo.

   - Julia will arrive on the first (1st) flight.

3. - Víctor se comió su tercer (3°) plato de ensalada.

   - Victor ate his third (3rd) plate of salad.

———————————

Exercises:

1.- Write the following numbers correctly in Spanish.

    a.- 2013 _____

    b.- 99 _____

    c.- 14° _____

    d.- 127 _____

    e.- 6 _____

    f.- 20° _____

    g.- 44 _____

    h.- 538 _____

    i.- 8° _____

    j.- 3,570 _____

2.- Write the number corresponding to each word.

    a.- Trescientos veinticinco _____

    b.- Treinta y cuatro _____

    c.- Cuadragésimo tercero _____

    d.- Mil doscientos ochenta y nueve _____

    e.- Quinto _____

    f.- Diecinueve _____

    g.- Veintiocho _____

    h.- Doce _____

    i.- Mil novecientos sesenta y tres _____

    j.- Sexagésimo _____

3.- Solve the sums and respond by writing the results in words in Spanish.

    a.- 45 + 10 = _____

    b.- 285 - 200 = _____

c.- 2 x 8 = _____

d.- 1,237 + 4,528 = _____

e.- 20 x 5 = _____

f.- 25 - 25 = _____

g.- 56 - 52 = _____

h.- 30 + 22 = _____

i.- 5.213 + 4 = _____

j.- 3 x 3 = _____

4.- Select the corresponding figure or words from the column on the right.

a.- 19	1.- Trigésimo
b.- 172	2.- 1.100
c.- 30°	3.- 75
d.- Mil cien	4.- Seiscientos dos
e.- 219	5.- Mil seiscientos seis
f.- Setenta y cinco	6.- 51°
g.- 1.000.000	7.- Diecinueve
h.- Quincuagésima primera	8.- Ciento setenta y dos
i.- 602	9.- Un millón
j.- 1606	10.- doscientos diecinueve

5.- Enter the missing number

a.- 5_5 = Quinientos cinco

b.- _0° = Nonagésimo

c.- 9_ = Noventa y ocho

d.- 22_ = Doscientos veinticuatro

e.- _0 = Diez

f.- 7_° = Septuagésimo sexto

g.- 1_10 = Mil ochocientos diez

h.- _ = Uno

i.- 1_° = Decimoséptimo

j.- _9 = Veintinueve

Translations:

Translate the following sentences into English:

1. - Celebraremos este **veinticuatro de diciembre**.

_____

2. - Daniela cumple años el **dieciséis** de junio.

_____

3. - Judith vive en la casa número **doscientos diecinueve**.

_____

4. - Ellos llegaron en **quinto** lugar.

_____

5. - El juego terminó **tres** a **cero**.

_____

6. - El boleto de avión cuesta **ciento setenta dólares**.

_____

7. - Visitamos el museo en la calle **trece**.

_____

8. - La pizza nos costó **doce** dólares.

_____

9. - Ganó su **primer** festival de música.

_____

10. - Vamos a la oficina del **decimoséptimo** piso.

_____

Story:

Rebecca es una **profesora** de matemáticas. Desde que era una niña **pequeña** le han gustado los números. Pero, cuando creció, Rebecca pensó que no le gustaría ser **profesora**. Ella pensó que no le gustaría trabajar con niños **pequeños**. Pero ese fue el primer trabajo que consiguió. Tendría que darle **clases** de matemáticas a un **salón** de veinticinco niños y niñas. Podría ser una experiencia muy interesante. Podría cambiarle la **vida** a Rebecca. Empezando por cambiar su forma de pensar.

La primera semana, Rebecca se dio cuenta de que el trabajo era más **complicado** de lo que pensaba. Había diez niños muy, muy inteligentes. Pero también había unos quince niños muy, muy **traviesos**. A la joven **profesora** le pareció muy difícil controlar a más de veinte niños al mismo tiempo. Pero, durante el segundo mes de dar **clases**, sucedió un **cambio**. Rebecca fue muy **feliz** al descubrir que los niños estaban aprendiendo, que ella les estaba cambiando la **vida**, y ellos también le cambiaban la **vida** a ella. Todos eran más felices porque aprendían juntos.

Vocabulary List:

1. Profesora – Teacher
2. Pequeña/Pequeños – Little
3. Clases – Classes
4. Salón – Classroom
5. Pensar – Think
6. Complicado – Complicated
7. Traviesos – Naughty
8. Cambio – Change
9. Feliz – Happy
10. Vida – Life

Translated Story:

Rebecca is a maths **teacher**. She has liked numbers since she was a **little** girl. But, when she grew up, Rebecca thought that she wouldn't like to be a **teacher.** She thought that she wouldn't like to work with **little** children. But that was the first job that she got. She would have to give maths **classes** to a **classroom** of twenty-five boys and girls. It could be a very interesting experience. It could change Rebecca's **life.** Starting with changing her way of thinking.

The first week, Rebecca realized that the job was more **complicated** than she thought. There were ten very, very intelligent children. But there were also fifteen very, very **naughty** children. The young **teacher** found it very difficult to control more than twenty children at the same time. But, during the second month of giving **classes**, a **change** happened. Rebecca was very **happy** to discover that the children were learning, that she was changing their lives and they were changing her **life** too. They were all happier because they were learning together.

Questions:

1. ¿De qué daba clases Rebecca? _____

   What classes does Rebecca teach?

2. ¿Cuál fue el primer trabajo de Rebecca? _____

   What was Rebecca's first job?

3. ¿Cuántos niños eran muy inteligentes? _____

   How many children were very intelligent?

4. ¿Cómo eran los otros quince niños?_____

   How were the other fifteen children?

5. ¿Cuándo sucedió un cambio? _____

   When did a change happen?

6. ¿Por qué todos eran felices? _____

   Why were they all happy?

Answers:

1. a.- dos mil trece
   b.- noventa y nueve
   c.- decimocuarto
   d.- ciento veintisiete
   e.- seis
   f.- vigésimo
   g.- cuarenta y cuatro
   h.- quinientos treinta y ocho
   i.- octavo
   j.- tres mil quinientos setenta

2. a.- 325
   b.- 34
   c.- 43°
   d.- 1289
   e.- 5°
   f.- 19
   g.- 28
   h.- 12
   i.- 1963
   j.- 60°

3. a.- cincuenta y cinco
   b.- ochenta y cinco
   c.- dieciséis
   d.- cinco mil setecientos sesenta y cinco
   e.- cien

f.- cero

g.- cuatro

h.- cincuenta y dos

i.- cinco mil doscientos diecisiete

j.- nueve

4. a.- 7

b.- 8

c.- 1

d.- 2

e.- 10

f.- 3

g.- 9

h.- 6

i.- 4

j.- 5

5. a.- 0

b.- 9

c.- 8

d.- 4

e.- 1

f.- 6

g.- 8

h.- 1

i.- 7

j.- 2

Translations:

1. - We will celebrate this **24th of December**.
2. - Daniela's birthday is on the **sixteenth** of June.
3. - Judith lives in house number **two hundred and nineteen**.
4. - They came in **fifth** place.
5. - The game ended **three** to **zero**.
6. - The plane ticket costs **one hundred and seventy** dollars.
7. - We visited the museum on the **thirteenth** street.
8. - The pizza cost us **twelve** dollars.
9. - He won his **first** music festival.
10. - Let's go to the office on the **seventeenth** floor.

Story:

1. Matemáticas. – Maths.
2. Profesora – Teacher.
3. Diez. – Ten.
4. Traviesos. – Naughty.
5. En el segundo mes. – In the second month.
6. Porque aprendían juntos. – Because they were learning together.

Chapter 4

<u>COLORS</u>

It's time to add a little color to life! And to learning, because in this chapter, we are going to review the colors in Spanish. By the end of this chapter, you will be able to identify, name, and write all the colors of the rainbow in Spanish.

Let's make a start:

Amarillo = Yellow

Azul = Blue

Rojo = Red

Morado = Purple

Naranja = Orange

Verde = Green

Blanco = White

Negro = Black

Gris = Gray

Marrón = Brown

Rosado = Pink

<u>Gender and number</u>:

In Spanish, the colors that end in a vowel change to correspond with the gender of noun they are describing (e.g., **amarillo/amarilla, rojo/roja**) except for green, which stays the same for both genders. The colors blue, gray and brown are also written the same when describing masculine and feminine nouns.

Plurals are made by adding **s** to the colors that end in a vowel (e.g., **verdes, blancos**) and **es** to the other colors. For example, blue as a plural is **azules**, gray is **grises** and brown is **marrones**.

<u>Examples:</u>

1. - Mi esposa tiene ojos **verdes**.

    - My wife has **green** eyes.

2. - No me gusta usar ropa **amarilla**.

    - I don't like wearing **yellow** clothes.

3. -¿Es cierto que el **rojo** enfurece a los toros?

    - Is it true that **red** infuriates bulls?

_____

Exercises:

1.- Complete the following sentences with the corresponding color in Spanish.

    1.1.- Los vestidos de las novias tradicionalmente son _____.

    1.2.- La grama del campo de golf era _____ y muy cuidada.

    1.3.- Compramos manzanas _____ y verdes.

    1.4.- Hoy el cielo amaneció despejado y de un _____ intenso.

    1.5.- Mi tía respeto el luto vistiendo sólo ropa _____ por   un

       año.

    1.6.- La _____ espuma de la leche rebosaba el vaso.

    1.7.- La camisa se manchó de _____ por la sangre de su herida.

    1.8.- José le dio un golpe que le dejo el ojo _____.

    1.9.- Llevaba un feo pantalón del mismo color _____ de la madera.

    1.10.- Las bananas maduras son _____.

2.- Write the corresponding color in Spanish.

    2.1.- Pink =   _____

    2.2.- Gray =   _____

    2.3.- White =   _____

    2.4.- Blue =   _____

    2.5.- Black =   _____

    2.6.- Yellow = _____

    2.7.- Red =   _____

    2.8.- Green =   _____

    2.9.- Purple =   _____

    2.10.- Orange = _____

3.- Select the corresponding color from the options in the right column.

3.1.- Brown	A.- Pink
3.2.- Verde	B.- Red
3.3.- Rosado	C.- White
3.4.- Yellow	D.- Gray
3.5.- Rojo	E.- Naranja
3.6.- Azul	F.- Marrón
3.7.- Blanco	G.- Negro
3.8.- Black	H.- Blue
3.9.- Gris	I.- Amarillo
3.10.- Orange	J.- Green

4.- Write the corresponding color in Spanish.

4.1.- COLOR (red)_____

4.2.-   _____

4.3.- COLOR (green)_____

4.4.- COLOR (Blue) _____

4.5.- COLOR (violet)_____

4.6.- COLOR (black)_____

4.7.- COLOR (orange)_____

4.8.- COLOR (red)_____

4.9.- COLOR (blue) _____

4.10.- COLOR (grey)_____

5.- Select the correct option.

     5.1.- Green

     a.- azul

     b.- rojo

     c.- verde

     5.2.- Brown

     a.- marrón

     b.- amarillo

     c.- gis

     5.3.- Pink

     a.- negro

     b.- rosado

     c.- azul

     5.4.- Gris

     a.- blue

     b.- white

     c.- gray

     5.5.- Rojo

     a.- orange

     b.- red

     c.- pink

     5.6.- Blanco

     a.- black

     b.- green

c.- white

5.7.- Yellow

a.- amarillo

b.- azul

c.- anaranjado

5.8.- Negro

a.- blue

b.- black

c.- yellow

5.9.- Purple

a.- morado

b.- anaranjado

c.- marrón

5.10.- Orange

a.- amarillo

b.- azul

c.- naranja

Translations:

Translate the following sentences into English:

1. - Su esposo le regaló rosas **rojas** en su aniversario.

   _____

2. - Mi casa se reconocía a la distancia, con paredes **verdes** y puertas **marrones**.

   _____

3. - Julio tenía un hermoso caballo **negro** de larga crin.

   _____

4. - Ana lucía muy bien con su vestido **verde**.

   _____

5. - Escribía todo lo que pasaba en su desgastado cuaderno **azul**.

   _____

6. - Cuando está enojada sus ojos cambian de **marrón** claro a **verde** intenso.

   _____

7. - ¡**Blanco, blanco**! ¡Quiero todas las paredes pintadas de **blanco**!

   _____

8. - Mi gata tuvo cuatro gatitos - todos de rayas **negras** y **grises**.

   _____

9. - No estaba seguro de querer comprar un carro **rojo**.

   _____

10. - Si es niña la manta **rosada**, si nace varón será la manta **azul**.

    _____

Story:

Mariana es una **artista**. Desde que era pequeña había demostrado un **talento** por el arte. Sus **dibujos** eran mucho más avanzados que los de los demás niños. Ella aprendió los nombres de los colores rojo, amarillo, y azul, antes que los nombres de sus propios **hermanos**. Al crecer, Mariana pasaba la mayor parte de su tiempo pintando y dibujando. Su color **favorito** era el verde. Cuando cumplió dieciséis años, pasó muchas horas pintando un hermoso bosque verde. Esa pintura terminó en un museo, y le consiguió a Mariana un puesto es una escuela de arte.

La joven **artista** tenía mucho que **aprender**. Ella sabía cómo **crear** hermosos colores morados y anaranjados. Pero sus profesores le enseñaron técnicas nuevas. Mariana podía hacer bellos dibujos en blanco y negro, pero sus nuevos profesores le explicaron cómo hacer **sombras** grises. El color más **lindo** de todos es el rosado, pero estudiando mucho, Mariana aprendió a **crear** cosas hermosas incluso **usando** solo el color marrón.

Vocabulary List:

1. Artista – Artist
2. Talento – Talent
3. Dibujos – Drawings
4. Hermanos – Siblings
5. Favorito – Favorite
6. Aprender – Learn
7. Crear – Create
8. Sombras – Shadows
9. Lindo – Pretty
10. Usando – Using

Translated Story:

Mariana is an **artist**. Since she was little, she had shown a **talent** for art. Her **drawings** were much more advanced than those of the other children. She learned the names of the colours red, yellow and blue before she learned the names of her own **siblings.** Growing up, Mariana used to spend the best part of her time painting and drawing. Her **favorite** color was green. When she turned sixteen years old, she spent many hours painting a beautiful green forest. That painting ended up in a museum, and it won Mariana a place in an art school.

The young **artist** had a lot to **learn.** She knew how to **create** beautiful purple and orange colors. But her teachers taught her new techniques. Mariana could do beautiful drawings in black and white, but her new teachers explained to her how to make gray **shadows**. The **prettiest** color of all is pink, but studying a lot, Mariana learned how to create beautiful things even only **using** the color brown.

Questions:

1. ¿Para qué tenía talento Mariana? _____

   What talent did Mariana have?

2. ¿Qué colores aprendió primero? _____

   Which colors did she learn first?

3. ¿Cuál es su color favorito? _____

   What is her favorite color?

4. ¿Qué pintó Mariana usando el color verde? _____

   What did Mariana paint using the color green?

5. ¿De qué color eran las sombras? _____

   What color were the shadows?

6. ¿Cuál es el color más lindo? _____

   What's the prettiest color?

Answers:

1.1.- blancos

1.2.- verde

1.3.- rojas

1.4.- azul

1.5.- negra

1.6.- blanca

1.7.- rojo

1.8.- morado

1.9.- marrón

1.10.- amarillas

2.1.- Rosado

2.2.- Gris

2.3.- Blanco

2.4.- Azul

2.5.- Negro

2.6.- Amarillo

2.7.- Rojo

2.8.- Verde

2.9.- Morado

2.10.- Naranja

3.1.- F

3.2.- J

3.3.- A

3.4.- I

3.5.- B

3.6.- H

3.7.- C

3.8.- G

3.9.- D

3.10.- E

4.1.- rojo

4.2.- amarillo

4.3.- verde

4.4.- azul

4.5.- morado

4.6.- negro

4.7.- naranja

4.8.- rojo

4.9.- azul

4.10.- gris

5.1.- c

5.2.- a

5.3.- b

5.4.- c

5.5.- b

5.6.- c

5.7.- a

5.8.- b

5.9.- a

5.10.- c

Translations:

1.   – Her husband gave her **red** roses on their anniversary.

2.   – My house was recognizable from a distance, with **green** walls and **brown** doors.

3.   – Julio had a beautiful **black** horse with a long mane.

4.   – Ana looked very good in her **green** dress.

5.   – He wrote everything that happened in his worn **blue** notebook.

6.   – When she is angry her eyes change from light **brown** to intense **green**.

7.   – **White, white!** I want all the walls painted **white**!

8.   – My cat had four kittens – all with **black** and **gray** stripes.

9.   – I wasn't sure I wanted to buy a **red** car.

10. – If it is a girl, the **pink** blanket, if a boy is born, it will be the **blue** blanket.

Story:

1. Para el arte. – For art.
2. Rojo, amarillo y azul. – Red, yellow and blue.
3. Verde. – Green.
4. Un bosque. – A forest.
5. Gris – Gray.
6. Rosado – Pink.

Chapter 5
DAYS OF THE WEEK

Do you know what day it is today? Good! Say it in Spanish, because in this chapter we are going to study the days of the week, so that when you visit Spain, Central, and South America you will be able to say and write what day it is. Without further delay, the seven days of the week are:

Monday	- lunes
Tuesday	- martes
Wednesday	- miércoles
Thursday	- jueves
Friday	- viernes
Saturday	- sábado
Sunday	- domingo

And remember that:

week	- semana
day	- día
weekend	- fin de semana

The days of the week are written entirely in lowercase in Spanish. Public holidays are called **días feriados** (Latin American Spanish) or **días festivos** (Castilian Spanish), and are days to celebrate an important event or date where people normally do not go to work or school (good, right?). The **fin de semana** is made up of Saturday and Sunday. Generally, the articles **El** and **Los** are used before mentioning the day.

Examples:

1. – El próximo **martes** es **día feriado**.
   - Next **Tuesday** is a **holiday**.

2. – Este **fin de semana** me toca trabajar **el sábado**, pero descansaré **el domingo**.

   - This **weekend** I have to work on **Saturday,** but I will rest on **Sunday**.

3. – Voy a marcar todos **los viernes** que son **feriados** en mi calendario.

   - I will mark all **Fridays** that are **holidays** on my calendar.

If you want to know what day it is, you can ask: **¿Qué día es hoy?** And the correct way to answer is: **Hoy es lunes**. To adapt this question and its answer in time, you must change the verb to **fue** (past) and **será** (future).

- **Hoy** – Today
- **Mañana** – Tomorrow
- **Ayer** – Yesterday
- **Pasado mañana** – the day after tomorrow
- **Antes de ayer** – the day before yesterday

Examples:
1. – P: ¿Qué día **es** hoy? R: Hoy **es** miércoles.

   - Q: What day **is it** today? A: Today **is** Wednesday.

2. – P: ¿Qué día **fue** ayer? R: Ayer **fue** martes.

   - Q: What day **was it** yesterday? A: Yesterday **was** Tuesday.

3. – P: ¿Qué día **será** mañana? R: Mañana **será** jueves.

   - Q: What day **will** it **be** tomorrow? A: Tomorrow **will be** Thursday.

———————————

Exercises:

1.- Fill in the missing day in Spanish.

      1.1.- Pasado mañana es _____, hoy es martes.

      1.2.- _____, martes, miércoles

      1.3.- viernes, _____, domingo

      1.4.- Hoy es jueves, mañana es _____.

      1.5.- lunes, martes, _____

      1.6.- sábado, _____, lunes

      1.7.- Hoy es _____, mañana es sábado.

      1.8.- Ayer fue _____, hoy es lunes.

      1.9.- miércoles, _____, viernes

      1.10.- miércoles, jueves, _____

2.- Answer true (V = **Verdad**) or false (F = **Falso**).

      2.1.- In Spanish, Monday is written as lunes.   _____

      2.2.- If today is martes, tomorrow is jueves.   _____

      2.3.- Today is sábado. The day after tomorrow is domingo.   _____

      2.4.- In Spanish, Friday is written as jueves.   _____

      2.5.- In Spanish, Sunday is written as domingo.   _____

      2.6.- Yesterday was miércoles, tomorrow is jueves.   _____

      2.7.- Tomorrow is jueves, the day before yesterday was sábado.   _____

      2.8.- The weekend is viernes and sábado.   _____

      2.9.- The first day of the week is miércoles.   _____

      2.10.- If tomorrow is jueves, yesterday was martes.   _____

3.- Select the correct option.

3.1.- El fin de semana es:

a.- viernes y sábado

b.- sábado y domingo

c.- domingo y lunes

3.2.- Tuesday en español es:

a.- martes

b.- jueves

c.- lunes

3.3.- Si hoy es viernes, pasado mañana es:

a.- domingo

b.- lunes

c.- miércoles

3.4.- El cuarto día de la semana es:

a.- viernes

b.- miércoles

c.- jueves

3.5.- Saturday en español es:

a.- viernes

b.- sábado

c.- domingo

3.6.- Si ayer fue domingo, pasado mañana es:

a.- martes

b.- miércoles

c.- viernes

3.7.- El séptimo día de la semana es:

a.- sábado

b.- viernes

c.- domingo

3.8.- Wednesday en español es:

a.- miércoles

b.- jueves

c.- martes

3.9.- Thursday en español es:

a.- lunes

b.- miércoles

c.- jueves

3.10.- Hoy es lunes, antes de ayer fue:

a.- domingo

b.- viernes

c.- sábado

4.- In the following word lists, underline the day of the week.

    4.1.- hola, diecisiete, miércoles, rojo

    4.2.- bienvenido, cuatro, adiós, martes

    4.3.- domingo, gracias, morado, treinta

    4.4.- disculpe, lunes, amarillo, cinco

    4.5.- veinte, bienvenido, viernes, verde

4.6.- adiós, martes, azul, doce

4.7.- jueves, cincuenta, gris, perdón

4.8.- disculpe, anaranjado, sábado, siete

4.9.- nueve, lunes, mañana, gracias

4.10.- adiós, dieciocho, ayer, domingo

5.- Complete the following sentences.

5.1.- El quinto día de la semana es el _____.

5.2.- Tuesday en español se escribe _____.

5.3.- Si hoy es miércoles, mañana será _____.

5.4.- Si ayer fue jueves, hoy es _____.

5.5.- El tercer día de la semana es el _____.

5.6.- Monday en español se escribe _____.

5.7.- El sexto día de la semana es el _____.

5.8.- Saturday en español se escribe _____.

5.9.- Si antes de ayer fue viernes, hoy es _____.

5.10.- Los días del fin de semana son _____ y _____.

Translations:

Translate the following sentences into English:

1.- Mi hija nació un **martes** en la mañana.

_____

2.- El **miércoles** pasan mi programa favorito en tv.

_____

3.- El **lunes** hay reunión en el departamento y el **jueves** una conferencia.

_____

4.- La Dra. Judith pasa consulta los **lunes**, **miércoles** y **viernes**.

_____

5.- El día favorito de Daniela es el **domingo** porque duerme hasta tarde.

_____

6.- Tenemos entrenamiento los **martes** y **jueves**. El **domingo** hay partido.

_____

7.- Julio y Miguel salen todos los **viernes** a tomar una copa.

_____

8.- El vuelo sale el **jueves** en la tarde.

_____

9.- La reunión del **martes** fue pospuesta para el **jueves**.

_____

10.- Este **sábado** trabajaremos de voluntarios en el refugio de perros.

_____

Story:

A todos nos gusta ir a **comer** a restaurantes. Son **lugares** muy **especiales**, donde podemos ir a pasar un buen rato y **comer** deliciosos platos de comida. Sin embargo, **trabajar** en un restaurante no es nada sencillo. Usualmente, tenemos que **trabajar** de lunes a viernes, y podemos **descansar** el fin de semana. Y tal vez **descansar** incluye ir a un restaurante. Así que para las personas que **trabajan** en estos **lugares**, los días más ocupados son sábados y domingos, los días en los que el resto de nosotros **descansamos**. Esto **explica** por qué a veces vemos que los restaurantes están cerrados los lunes, martes, o miércoles. Todos necesitamos **descansar**.

Dentro de un restaurante, cada día es interesante, y cada día es un desafío. Por **ejemplo**, si ayer prepararon la mejor pizza, y hoy hicieron una muy buena ensalada, mañana la estrella del menú será el postre. Así pasan todas las semanas. Si antes de ayer se destacaron con la sopa del día, pasado mañana probablemente preparen un sorprendente pollo. La **verdad** es que las cocinas de los restaurantes son **lugares** mágicos. Todos los **cocineros** son muy talentosos, y tienen muchas tareas que hacer. Algunos se dedican a los vegetales los jueves, y otros **trabajan** las carnes los viernes. Todos los restaurantes son diferentes, tienen sus **secretos**, y nosotros los apreciamos.

Vocabulary:

1. Comer – Eat
2. Especial/es – Special
3. Trabajar – Work
4. Descansamos/Descansar – Rest
5. Lugar/es – Place/s
6. Explica – Explain
7. Ejemplo – Example
8. Verdad – Truth
9. Cocineros – Chefs
10. Secretos – Secrets

Translated Story:

We all like to go to **eat** at restaurants. They are very **special places**, where we can go to have a good time and **eat** delicious dishes of food. However, to work in a restaurant isn't at all easy. Usually, we have to **work** from Monday to Friday, and we can **rest** at the weekend. And maybe '**rest**' includes going to a restaurant. So, for the people who **work** in these places, the busiest days are Saturdays and Sundays, the days in which the rest of us **rest**. This **explains** why we sometimes see that restaurants are closed on Mondays, Tuesdays or Wednesdays. We all need to **rest.**

Inside a restaurant, every day is interesting, and every day is a challenge. For **example,** if yesterday they prepared the best pizza, ad today they made a very good salad, the dessert will be the star of the menu tomorrow. That's how all the weeks pass. If the day before yesterday they stood out with the soup of the day, the day after tomorrow they will probably prepare an amazing chicken. The **truth** is that restaurant kitchens are magical **places**. All the **chefs** are very talented, and they have many tasks to do. Some of them are dedicated to the vegetables on Thursdays, and others work with the meat on Fridays. All the restaurants are different, they have their secrets and we appreciate them.

Questions:

1. ¿Cómo es trabajar en un restaurante?_____

   What is it like to work in a restaurant?

2. ¿Cuáles son los días más ocupados en un restaurante? _____

   What are the busiest days in a restaurant?

3. ¿Cuándo cierran los restaurantes?_____

   When do restaurants close?

4. ¿Quiénes necesitan descansar?_____

   Who needs to rest?

5. ¿Qué cocinaron ayer? _____

   What did they cook yesterday?

6. ¿Cuándo trabajan con vegetales y carnes? _____

   When do they work with vegetables and meats?

Answers:

1.1.- jueves

1.2.- lunes

1.3.- sábado

1.4.- viernes

1.5.- miércoles

1.6.- domingo

1.7.- viernes

1.8.- domingo

1.9.- jueves

1.10.- viernes

2.1.- V

2.2.- F

2.3.- F

2.4.- F

2.5.- V

2.6.- F

2.7.- V

2.8.- F

2.9.- F

2.10.- V

3.1.- b

3.2.- a

3.3.- a

3.4.- c

3.5.- b

3.6.- b

3.7.- c

3.8.- a

3.9.- c

3.10.- c

4.1.- miércoles

4.2.- martes

4.3.- domingo

4.4.- lunes

4.5.- viernes

4.6.- martes

4.7.- jueves

4.8.- sábado

4.9.- lunes

4.10.- domingo

5.1.- viernes

5.2.- martes

5.3.- jueves

5.4.- viernes

5.5.- miércoles

5.6.- lunes

5.7.- sábado

5.8.- sábado

5.9.- domingo

5.10.- sábado / domingo

Translations:

1. - My daughter was born on a **Tuesday** morning.
2. - On **Wednesday** they show my favorite TV show.
3. - On **Monday** there is a meeting in the department and on **Thursday** a conference.
4. - Dr. Judith has a consultation on **Monday**, **Wednesday** and **Friday**.
5. - Daniela's favorite day is **Sunday** because she sleeps late.
6. - We have training on **Tuesday** and **Thursday**. On **Sunday** there is a game.
7. - Julio and Miguel go out every **Friday** to have a drink.
8. - The flight leaves on **Thursday** afternoon.
9. - **Tuesday's** meeting was postponed to **Thursday**.
10. - This **Saturday we will** work as volunteers in the dog shelter.

Story:

1. No es nada fácil. – It's not easy.
2. sábados y domingos. – Saturdays and Sundays.
3. lunes, martes o miércoles. – Mondays, Tuesdays or Wednesdays.
4. Todos. - Everyone.
5. Pizza. – Pizza.
6. jueves y viernes. – Thursdays and Fridays.

Chapter 6
MONTHS OF THE YEAR

In this chapter, we are going to study the months of the year. You will notice that they are written similarly in English and Spanish. This is because both languages take the names of the months from the Roman calendar which is written in Latin. This is sure to facilitate the learning process.

So, let's start! The months of the year in Spanish are:

January	- enero
February	- febrero
March	- marzo
April	- abril
May	- mayo
June	- junio
July	- julio
August	- agosto
September	- septiembre
October	- octubre
November	- noviembre
December	- diciembre

It's also useful to know:

month	- mes
year	- año

Just the same as the days of the week, the months are written in lower case unless they are part of names of festivities, historical events, or names of streets or buildings.

<u>Examples</u>:

1. - Mi esposa cumple años en diciembre.

    - My wife has a birthday in December.

2. - Te invito a comer en mi casa el Viernes Santo.

    - I invite you to eat at my house on Good Friday.

3. - Los novios se encontraron en la Plaza 5 de Mayo.

    - The couple met in Plaza 5 de Mayo.

4. - Comenzaron las obras en el mes de febrero.

    - The works began in the month of February.

Exercises:

1.- In the following word lists, underline the month of the year.

      1.1.- lunes, amarillo, hola, agosto

      1.2.- perdón, septiembre, azul, cuatro

      1.3.- julio, siete, adiós, domingo

      1.4.- jueves, sábado, mayo, veinte

      1.5.- morado, miércoles, marzo, disculpe

      1.6.- noviembre, martes, décimo, adiós

      1.7.- viernes, negro, ochenta, octubre

      1.8.- gracias, trigésimo, abril, chao

      1.9.- bienvenido, diciembre, domingo, buenas

      1.10.- junio, jueves, rojo, adiós

2.- Complete the following sentences with the correct month in Spanish.

      2.1.- Después de febrero viene el mes de _____.

      2.2.- El primer mes del año es _____.

      2.3.- La Navidad se celebra en _____.

      2.4.- Antes de julio está el mes de _____.

      2.5.- En español, November se escribe _____.

      2.6.- El octavo mes del año es _____.

      2.7.- En español, September se escribe _____.

      2.8.- Después de abril viene el mes de _____.

      2.9.- El décimo mes de año es _____.

      2.10.- Antes de mayo está el mes de _____.

3.- Select the corresponding month in Spanish from the column on the right.

      3.1.- April   A.- mayo

      3.2.- January   B.- junio

3.3.- October	C.- febrero
3.4.- August	D.- diciembre
3.5.- March	E.- octubre
3.6.- December	F.- abril
3.7.- February	G.- marzo
3.8.- June	H.- enero
3.9.- November	I.- noviembre
3.10.- May	J.- agosto

4.- Enter the months of the year that correspond in Spanish.

4.1.- 10th month: _____

4.2.- 2nd month: _____

4.3.- 12th month: _____

4.4.- 1st month: _____

4.5.- 7th month: _____

4.6.- 3rd month: _____

4.7.- 9th month: _____

4.8.- 5th month: _____

4.9.- 8th month: _____

4.10.- 4th month: _____

5.- Enter the missing months, maintaining chronological order.

5.1.- enero, _____, marzo

5.2.- junio, julio, _____

5.3.- _____, mayo, junio

5.4.- _____, noviembre, diciembre

5.5.- marzo, abril, _____

5.6.- agosto, _____, octubre

5.7.- mayo, junio, _____

5.8.- febrero, _____, abril

5.9.- septiembre, octubre, _____

5.10.- _____, febrero, marzo

Translations:

Translate the following sentences into English:

1.- Ellos se casaron una tarde de **junio**.

_____

2.- Ana me invitó a su casa para el 24 de **diciembre**.

_____

3.- Las clases iniciarán el 15 de **septiembre**.

_____

4.- En **abril** se celebra la independencia en mi país.

_____

5.- **Julio** y **agosto** son los meses más cálidos del año.

_____

6.- Antonio espera las lluvias de **junio** para iniciar la siembra.

_____

7.- Definitivamente **diciembre** es mi mes favorito.

_____

8.- Los primeros días de **enero** el hotel se llenaba de turistas.

_____

9.- **Febrero** es el mes más corto del año.

_____

10.- En **mayo** se encuentran las flores más hermosas en el mercado.

_____

Story:

Luego de haberse graduado de la **universidad**, Angelica decidió viajar por el mundo. Escogió doce países e hizo un plan para visitarlos todos en un año. El primer mes era enero y el país que escogió fue España. Era **invierno**, así que paso todo el mes usando un gran **abrigo**, y también **disfrutó** de buenos vinos. En febrero, Angelica **visitó** Francia. Aún hacía mucho **frío**, pero el país era aún más hermoso. Luego **llegó** marzo, y Angelica **llegó** a México, lo cual fue un gran cambio. Era mucho más cálido, y Angelica pudo ir a la **playa**.

El siguiente mes fue abril, y Angelica viajó a Argentina. **Disfrutó** mucho el país e **incluso** llegó cerca de la Antártida, donde observó pingüinos. En mayo, Angelica **llegó** hasta Marruecos, y fue una experiencia totalmente diferente. En junio, Angelica **visitó** Jamaica, y dijo que le cambió la vida. Al igual que su viaje a Japón en julio. El mes de agosto la llevó a Australia, donde **incluso** trabajó un poco para seguir pagando su viaje cómodamente. En septiembre fue a Suiza, y en octubre solo se le ocurrió ir a Estados Unidos a **disfrutar** Halloween. Finalmente, en noviembre, Angelica visitó Noruega, y en diciembre terminó su viaje en Dinamarca.

Vocabulary:

1. Universidad – University
2. Viajar – Travel
3. Invierno – Winter
4. Abrigo – Coat
5. Visitó – Visited
6. Frío – Cold
7. Llegó – Arrived
8. Playa – Beach
9. Incluso – Even
10. Disfrutó – Enjoyed

Translated Story:

After having graduated from **university**, Angelica decided to travel the world. She chose twelve countries and made a plan to visit them all in a year. The first month was January and the country that she chose was Spain. It was **winter**, so she spent the whole month wearing a big **coat**, and she also **enjoyed** some good wines. In February, Angelica **visited** France. It was still very **cold**, but the country was even more beautiful. Then March **arrived**, and Angelica **arrived** at Mexico, which was a big change. It was much warmer, and Angelica was able to go to the **beach**.

The next month was April, and Angelica traveled to Argentina. She really **enjoyed** the country and **even** got close to Antarctica, where she saw penguins. In May, Angelica **arrived** at Morocco, and it was a totally different experience. In June, Angelica **visited** Jamaica, and she said that it changed her life. The same as her trip to Japan in July. The month of August took her to Australia, where she **even** worked a little to continue comfortably paying for her journey. In September she went to Switzerland, and in October she only thought of going to the United States to **enjoy** Halloween. Finally, in November, Angelica visited Norway, and in December she finished her trip in Denmark.

Questions:

1. ¿Cuántos países visitó Angelica? _____

   How many countries did Angelica visit?

2. ¿Cuál fue el segundo país que visitó?_____

   Which was the second country that she visited?

3. ¿En qué mes fue a la playa Angelica? _____

   In what month did Angelica go to the beach?

4. ¿A dónde fue Angelica en Mayo? _____

   Where did Angelica go in May?

5. ¿En qué mes Angelica trabajó un poco?_____

   In what month did Angelica work a little bit?

6. ¿En qué mes y en qué país terminó el viaje? _____

   In what month and what country did the trip finish?

Answers:

1.1.- agosto

1.2.- septiembre

1.3.- julio

1.4.- mayo

1.5.- marzo

1.6.- noviembre

1.7.- octubre

1.8.- abril

1.9.- diciembre

1.10.- junio

2.1.- marzo

2.2.- enero

2.3.- diciembre

2.4.- junio

2.5.- noviembre

2.6.- agosto

2.7.- septiembre

2.8.- mayo

2.9.- octubre

2.10.- abril

3.1.- F

3.2.- H

3.3.- E

3.4.- J

3.5.- G

3.6.- D

3.7.- C

3.8.- B

3.9.- I

3.10.- A

4.1.- octubre

4.2.- febrero

4.3.- diciembre

4.4.- enero

4.5.- julio

4.6.- marzo

4.7.- septiembre

4.8.- mayo

4.9.- agosto

4.10.- abril

5.1.- febrero

5.2.- agosto

5.3.- abril

5.4.- octubre

5.5.- mayo

5.6.- septiembre

5.7.- julio

5.8.- marzo

5.9.- noviembre

5.10.- enero

Translations:

1. - They got married one afternoon in **June**.

2. - Ana invited me to her home on the 24th of **December**.

3. - Classes will start on **September** 15th.

4. - In **April** independence is celebrated in my country.

5. - **July** and **August** are the warmest months of the year.

6. - Antonio waits for the **June** rains to start sowing.

7. **- December** is definitely my favorite month.

8. - The first days of **January** the hotel was full of tourists.

9. - **February** is the shortest month of the year.

10. - In **May** you will find the most beautiful flowers on the market.

Story:

1. Doce. – Twelve.

2. Francia. – France.

3. México. – Mexico.

4. Marruecos. – Morocco.

5. Australia. – Australia.

6. Dinamarca en diciembre. – Denmark in December,

Chapter 7
<u>THE TIME</u>

Do you know what time it is? You already know the days of the week and the months of the year, so now it's time to learn the time in Spanish. Let's see how to ask the time, how to tell someone the time, and look at some recommendations that will allow us to arrive on time in Spanish.

In Spanish, we can use the analog format of 0 to 12 hours using the abbreviations am (before meridiem or before noon) and pm (post meridiem or after noon). The meridiem is noon / midday. It is more common to see am and pm written than spoken. The digital format of 0 to 24 hours is used for reports, programming, and in scientific contexts. As we already know the numbers in Spanish (*Chapter 3*) from 0 to 24, for this topic we will use the analog format of 0 to 12 hours.

To ask and tell the time, the verb **ser (to be) is used**. To ask, the third person singular (**es**) **is used: ¿Qué hora es?** Another more formal way is **¿Me puede decir la hora, por favor?** If you want to know the time of a specific event or moment, it will be **¿A que hora es...?** In this case, the answer is with **a la/ las…** To answer, the third person singular (**es**) is only used if it is about one o'clock (1) as it is singular. To answer when referring to the other hours (2, 3, 4…), we use the third person plural (**son**).

Examples:
1. - P: ¿Qué hora es?

    R: Es la una.

   - Q: What time is it?

    A: It's one o'clock.

2. - P: ¿Me puede decir la hora, por favor?

    R: Son las cinco.

    - Q: Can you tell me the time please?

    A: It's five o'clock.

3. - P: ¿Qué hora es?

    R: Son las diez en punto.

    - Q: What time is it?

    A: It's ten o'clock.

4. - P: ¿A qué hora es el juego?

    R: A las cinco en punto.

    - Q: What time is the game?

    A: At five o'clock.

For the exact hour (as shown in the previous examples), we can say o'clock in two ways.

Examples:

- 1:00 = It's one o'clock. - Es la una. / Es la una en punto.

- 5:00 = It's five o'clock. - Son las cinco. / Son las cinco en punto.

- 10:00 = It's ten o'clock. - Son las diez. / Son las diez en punto.

Sometimes we need to specify which part of the day we are talking about. In English, we might say am or pm but in Spanish, people tend to say the following:

Examples:

- 7:00am = It's seven o'clock **in the morning**. – Son las siete **de la mañana**.

- 3:00pm = It's three **in the afternoon**. – Son las tres **de la tarde**.

- 9:00pm = It's nine o'clock **in the evening/night**. – Son las nueve **de la noche**.

To answer with hours and minutes we use the conjunction **Y** in the case of the first 30 minutes. At 15 minutes we can use **"y cuarto"** (quarter past), and at 30 minutes we can use **"y media"** (half past). We can end with the word **"minutos"** or not.

Examples:

1. - 8:18 = Son las ocho y dieciocho.

    - 8:18 = It's eight eighteen.

2. - 3:15 = Son las tres y quince. / Son las tres y cuarto.

    - 3:15 = It's three fifteen. / It's quarter past three

3. - 1:20 = Es la una y veinte.

    - 1:20 = It's twenty past one.

4. - 4:30 = Son las cuatro y treinta. / Son las cuatro y media.

    - 4:30 = It's four thirty. / It's half past four.

5. - 11:16 = Son las once y dieciséis minutos.

    - 11:16 = It's sixteen minutes past eleven.

To answer the hour with minutes from 31 to 59, there are two ways, depending on if we are in Spain or in Latin America.

In Spain, it would be *The Next Hour* + **Menos** + *The Minutes Left*.

Examples:

1. - 7:35 = Son las ocho menos veinticinco minutos.

    - 7:35 = It's twenty-five minutes to eight.

2. - 8:40 = Son las nueve menos veinte.

    - 8:40 = It's twenty to nine.

3. -12:50 = Es la una menos diez.

    -12: 50 = It's ten to one.

In Latin America, it is *The Minutes Left* + **Para (la/las)** + *The Next Hour.*

    <u>Examples</u>:

1. - 7:35 = Son veinticinco minutos para las ocho.

    - 7:35 = It's twenty-five minutes to eight.

2. - 8:40 = Son veinte minutos para las nueve.

    - 8:40 = It's twenty minutes to nine.

3. - 12:50 = Son diez minutos para la una.

    - 12:50 = It's ten minutes to one.

In both places, for the hour and 45 minutes you can use **"(the next hour) menos cuarto"** (Spain) and **"un cuarto para la/las (the next hour)"** (Latin America).

    <u>Examples</u>:

1. - 6:45 = Son las siete menos quince minutos. / Son las siete menos cuarto. (España)

    - 6:45 = Son quince minutos para las siete. / Son un cuarto para las siete. (América Latina)

    - 6:45 = It's fifteen minutes to seven. / It's a quarter to seven.

2. - 2:45 = Son las tres menos quince. / Son las tres menos cuarto. (España)

    - 2:45 = Son quince para las tres. / Son un cuarto para las tres. (América Latina)

    - 2:45 = It's fifteen minutes to three. / It's a quarter to three.

———————

Exercises:

1.- Write the time in Spanish.

      1.1.- 8:10   _____

      1.2.- 4:25   _____

      1.3.- 7:50pm   _____

      1.4.- 1:00   _____

      1.5.- 3:45   _____

      1.6.- 9:15am   _____

      1.7.- 2:30   _____

      1.8.- 1:05pm   _____

      1.9.- 12:00   _____

      1.10.- 6:35am   _____

2.- Read and write the indicated hour in numbers.

      2.1.- Tres y diecisiete   _____

      2.2.- Nueve y media de la mañana   _____

      2.3.- Las dos en punto de la tarde   _____

      2.4.- Un cuarto para las cinco   _____

      2.5.- Seis y seis   _____

      2.6.- Siete menos diez   _____

      2.7.- Una y cuarto   _____

      2.8.- Ocho y doce de la noche   _____

      2.9.- Once menos un minuto   _____

      2.10.- Un cuarto para las cuatro   _____

3.- Correctly answer the question in Spanish with the time indicated in brackets.

    3.1.- ¿Qué hora es? (6:19) _____

    3.2.- ¿A qué hora sale el próximo tren? (3:30) _____

    3.3.- ¿Qué hora es? (1:05) _____

    3.4.- ¿Me puede decir la hora por favor? (2:00) _____

    3.5.- ¿Qué hora es? (4.00pm) _____

    3.6.- ¿A qué hora es la reunión? (7:45) _____

    3.7.- ¿Qué hora es? (10:20am) _____

    3.8.- ¿Qué hora es? (5:45) _____

    3.9.- ¿A qué hora es el juego? (11:10am) _____

    3.10.- ¿Me puede decir la hora por favor (3:04pm) _____

4.- Choose the correct time from the alternatives.

    4.1.- 7:10

    a.- Son las siete menos diez.

    b.- Son las ocho menos cincuenta.

    c.- Son las siete y diez.

    4.2.- 5:50

    a.- Son las seis menos diez.

    b.- Son las cinco y cinco.

    c.- Son las cinco menos diez.

    4.3.- 1:00

    a.- Son la una en punto.

    b.- Es la una en punto.

    c.- Son las diez en punto.

4.4.- 6:30

a.- Son las seis y cuarto.

b.- Son las siete menos treinta.

c.- Son las seis y media.

4.5.- 4:45

a.- Son las cuatro y cuarto.

b.- Son un cuarto para las cinco.

c.- Son un cuarto para las cuatro.

4.6.- 2:25

a.- Son las dos y veinticinco.

b.- Son las tres menos treinta y cinco.

c.- Son las dos y media.

4.7.- 8:40

a.- Son las nueve y veinte.

b.- Son las ocho menos veinte.

c.- Son veinte para las nueve.

4.8.- 3:15

a.- Son las tres y media.

b.- Son las tres y cuarto.

c.- Son las cinco y trece.

4.9.- 1:20

a.- Es la una y veinte.

b.- Es la una menos veinte.

c.- Son la una y veinte.

4.10.- 7:29

a.- Son las siete y media.

b.- Es la siete y veintinueve.

c.- Son las siete y veintinueve.

5.- Select the corresponding time from the right column.

5.1.- 3:52	A.- Son las seis y diecisiete.
5.2.- 8:10	B.- Son las once y treinta.
5.3.- Son las dos y cinco.	C.- Son las cuatro de la tarde.
5.4.- 6:17	D.- 2:00
5.5.- 4:00pm	E.- Son las nueve de la mañana.
5.6.- Es la una menos cuarto.	F.- 2:05
5.7.- Son las dos en punto.	G.- Son las cuatro menos ocho.
5.8.- 9:00am	H.- Son las doce y cinco minutos.
5.9.- 11:30	I.- 12:45
5.10.- 12:05	J.- Son las ocho y diez

Translations:

Translate the following sentences into English:

1.- Hoy vamos a almorzar **a la una de la tarde**.

_____

2.- La reunión de **las tres y media** fue cambiada para **las cinco y cuarto**.

_____

3.- Judith siempre llega al trabajo a **un cuarto para las siete**.

_____

4.- El bus llegó **a las nueve y veintisiete**.

_____

5.- -Ana: **¿Qué hora es?** _____

   -Marcos: Son **las ocho y diez.** _____

6.- El vuelo se retrasó y no saldrá antes de **las once y media**.

_____

7.- -Laura: **¿A qué hora nos vemos?** _____

   -Simón: **A las cuatro en punto.** _____

8.- Ella se levantó muy tarde, eran ya **las diez de la mañana**.

_____

9.- -Juan: **¿Me puede decir la hora por favor?** _____

   -Ramón: Sí, por supuesto. Son **las seis y cinco.** _____

10.- Los niños entran a clase **a las siete menos cuarto**.

_____

Story:

El día veinticinco de diciembre de cada año se celebra la **Navidad**. Millones de personas en todo el planeta celebran este día especial. Y uno de los **personajes** más reconocidos en relación a este día, es el **famoso** Santa Claus. En español también es conocido como San Nicolás, o Papá Noel. Se podría decir que es un hombre muy **ocupado**, y en **Navidad** tiene que trabajar las veinticuatro horas del día. A las doce en punto en Nueva Zelanda, Santa Claus ya está repartiendo **regalos**. Y cuando pregunta a los duendes "¿Qué hora es?" y ellos responden, "Son la una y treinta," ya Santa Claus debe estar terminando de entregar **regalos** en China.

A todos, cuando somos niños, nos dicen que tenemos que **dormir** temprano para **esperar** el **regalo** que trae Santa Claus. Ya sea a las siete y veinte, o a las ocho menos cuarto. Algunos duermen a las nueve y diez, y otros a las diez menos veinte. Los niños **grandes** tal vez se duerman a las once en punto. Pero todos pueden esperar un **regalo** de Santa Claus. Al menos, todos los niños buenos del mundo. Al **despertar**, a las seis, a las siete y cuarto, a las ocho y veinticinco, o a las diez menos veinte, todos tendrán sus **regalos** esperando bajo el **árbol** de **Navidad**.

Vocabulary:

1. Navidad – Christmas
2. Personaje – Character
3. Famoso – Famous
4. Ocupado – Busy
5. Regalos – Gifts
6. Dormir – Sleep
7. Grandes – Big
8. Esperar – Wait
9. Despertar – Wake
10. Árbol – Tree

Translated Story:

Christmas is celebrated every year on the twenty-fifth of December. Millions of people around the world celebrate this special day. And one of the most recognised **characters** in relation to this day, is the **famous** Santa Claus. In Spanish, he is also known as Saint Nicholas or Father Christmas. You could say that he is a very **busy** man, and at **Christmas** he has to work twenty-four hours a day. At twelve o'clock in New Zealand, Santa Claus is already handing out **gifts**. And when he asks the elves "What time is it?" and they respond, "It's one thirty," Santa Claus must be finishing delivering **gifts** in China.

All of us, when we are children, are told that we have to **sleep** early to **wait** for the **gift** that Santa Claus brings. Be it twenty past seven or a quarter to eight. Some sleep at ten past nine, and others at twenty to ten. The **big** kids perhaps go to sleep at eleven o'clock. But everyone can expect a **gift** from Santa Claus. At least, all the good children in the world. When they **wake**, at six, quarter past seven, twenty-five past eight, or at twenty to ten, they will all have their **gifts** waiting under the **Christmas tree.**

Questions:

1. ¿Cuándo se celebra Navidad? _____

   When is Christmas celebrated?

2. ¿Cómo es conocido Santa Claus en español? _____

   How is Santa Claus known in Spanish?

3. ¿A qué hora empieza a trabajar Santa Claus? _____

   What time does Santa Claus start work?

4. ¿Qué entrega Santa Claus? _____

   What does Santa Claus deliver?

5. ¿A qué hora se duermen los niños grandes? _____

   What time do the big kids go to sleep?

6. ¿Dónde nos esperan los regalos? _____

   Where are the gifts waiting for us?

Answers:

1.1.- Son las ocho y diez.

1.2.- Son las cuatro y veinticinco.

1.3.- Son las ocho menos diez de la noche. / Son las diez para las ocho de la noche.

1.4.- Es la una. / Es la una en punto.

1.5.- Son las cuatro menos cuarto. / Son un cuarto para las cuatro.

1.6.- Son las nueve y quince de la mañana. / Son las nueve y cuarto de la mañana.

1.7.- Son las dos y treinta. / Son las dos y media.

1.8.- Es la una y cinco de la tarde.

1.9.- Son las doce. / Son las doce en punto. (midday / noon / midnight)

1.10.- Son las siete menos veinticinco de la mañana. / Son las veinticinco para las siete de la mañana.

2.1.- 3:17

2.2.- 9:30

2.3.- 2:00

2.4.- 4:45

2.5.- 6:06

2.6.- 6:50

2.7.- 1:15

2.8.- 8:12

2.9.- 10:59

2.10.- 3:45

3.1.- Son las seis y diecinueve.

3.2.- A las tres y media.

3.3.- Es la una y cinco.

3.4.- Si, son las dos en punto.

3.5.- Son las cuatro de la tarde.

3.6.- A un cuarto para las ocho. / A las ocho menos cuarto.

3.7.- Son las diez y veinte minutos de la mañana.

3.8.- Son las seis menos cuarto. / Son un cuarto para las seis.

3.9.- A las once y diez de la mañana.

3.10.- Si, son las tres y cuatro de la tarde.

4.1.- c

4.2.- a

4.3.- b

4.4.- c

4.5.- b

4.6.- a

4.7.- c

4.8.- b

4.9.- a

4.10.- c

5.1.- G

5.2.- J

5.3.- F

5.4.- A

5.5.- C

5.6.- I

5.7.- D

5.8.- E

5.9.- B

5.10.- H

Translations:

1.- Today we are going to have lunch **at one in the afternoon**.

2.- The meeting at **half past three** was changed to **quarter past five**.

3.- Judith always arrives at work at **a quarter to seven**.

4.- The bus arrived **at nine twenty-seven**.

5.- -Ana: **What time is it?**

   -Marcos: It's **ten past eight**.

6.- The flight was delayed and will not leave before **eleven thirty**.

7.- -Laura: **What time do we meet?**

   -Simón: **At four o'clock**.

8.- She got up very late, it was already **ten in the morning**.

9.- -Juan: **Can you tell me the time please?**

         -Ramón: Yes, of course. It's **five past six**.

10.- The children enter class at **a quarter to seven**.

Story:

1. El veinticinco de diciembre. – The twenty-fifth of December.

2. San Nicolás o Papá Noél. – Saint Nicholas or Father Christmas.

3. A las doce en punto. – At twelve o'clock.

4. Regalos. – Gifts.

5. A las once en punto. – At eleven o'clock.

6. Bajo el árbol de Navidad. – Under the Christmas tree.

Chapter 8
THE DATE

To measure your progress in learning Spanish, it's important to keep a record or log of the themes you have covered and how long you have been studying. This involves recording the start date of each topic and what you have accomplished so far. What is better, when you finish this chapter, you will know how to say the date in Spanish.

We recommend you review the previous chapters on **numbers (3), days of the week (5) and months of the year (6)** as they will also be very useful when asking for, giving and writing the date.

In Spanish, it is recommended to use ascending order to give the date: **day, month, and year** (as in British English). The day and year are written in numbers and the month in letters (always remember to use lower case). The days are cardinal numbers (two, three, four) except for 1, which is ordinal - **primero**. Before the month and year use the preposition **de / del** (it is *customary to* use **de** until 1999 and from 2000 and onwards use **del**). If the day of the week is stated, then there is a comma (,). No periods or commas should be added to the figures for the year, unless they are written down and punctuation is necessary for what you are writing.

Examples:

1. - 27 de diciembre de 1967
   - 27th of December 1967

2. - Viernes, 22 de agosto del 2013
   - Friday, 22nd of August 2013

3. - Hoy es primero de agosto.

- Today is the first of August.

If you want to write the abbreviated date, only numbers are used, separating the day, month, and year with dashes, hyphens or dots.

4.   - 29-06-1996

5.   - 29/06/1996

6.   - 29.06.1996

Asking for, and giving someone the date.

To ask and give the date we can use the verb **estar** and also the verb **ser**.

With the verb **estar** we use the first-person plural (**estamos**) and the preposition **a**.

Examples:

1.   - P: ¿A qué día **estamos**? R: **Estamos a** 27 de febrero.
     - Q: What day are we on? A: We are on 27th February.

2.   - P: ¿A qué fecha estamos hoy? R: Hoy estamos a 18 de noviembre de 2018.
     - Q: What date is it today? A: Today is the 18th of November 2018.

3.   - P: ¿A cuánto estamos? R: Estamos a 15 de marzo.
     - Q: When are we? A: We are on 15th of March.

With the verb **ser** we use the third-person singular (**es**) without a preposition.

Examples:

1.   - P: ¿Qué día **es** hoy? R: Hoy **es** 27 de enero.
     - Q: What day is it today? A: Today is January 27.

2. - P: ¿Qué día es? R: Es martes.

   - Q: What day is it? A: It's Tuesday.

3. -P: ¿Qué fecha es hoy? R: Hoy es 21 de junio.

   -Q: What date is it today? A: Today is June 21.

With any other verb, the article **el** is used to give a specific date or day.

Examples:

1. - P: ¿Cuándo sale el vuelo a París? R: Sale **el** 15 de abril.

   - Q: When does the flight to Paris leave? A: It leaves on April 15.

2. - P: ¿Cuándo vamos a vernos? R: Nos veremos el sábado.

   - Q: When are we going to meet? A: We will meet on Saturday.

3. -P: ¿Qué día nos reuniremos con el jefe? R: Nos reuniremos el miércoles.

   -Q: What day will we meet with the boss? A: We will meet on Wednesday.

To talk about a month and / or year only, the preposition **en** is used.

Examples:

1. - Mi hija nació **en** junio.

   - My daughter was born in June.

2. - Me casé en 1996.

   - I got married in 1996.

3. - El negocio se vendió en 2013.

   - The business was sold in 2013.

———————

120

Exercises:

1.- Write these dates in Spanish.

    1.1.- 12-28-1963 (American English)

_____

    1.2.- 29-6-1996 (British English)

_____

    1.3.- year: 1998, day: 16, month: June

_____

    1.4.- day: 13, month: August, year: 2013

_____

    1.5.- 04-01-2016 (British English)

_____

    1.6.- month: 9, year: 2002, day: 25 (Monday)

_____

    1.7.- day: 21, month: 05, year: 2005

_____

    1.8.- year: 1994, day: 24 (Thursday), month: 02

_____

    1.9.- 04-11-1935 (American English)

_____

    1.10.- month: 12, day: 31, year: 2000

_____

2.- Answer the following questions in Spanish according to the date indicated in brackets.

    2.1.- ¿Qué día es hoy? (19-02)

_____

2.2.- ¿A qué fecha estamos? (24-09)

_____

2.3.- ¿Qué día es? (Tuesday)

_____

2.4.- ¿Cuándo sale tu nuevo libro? (12-10-2021 – British English)

_____

2.5.- ¿A cuánto estamos? (Monday 15)

_____

2.6.- ¿Qué fecha es hoy? (17-11)

_____

2.7.- ¿Qué día es mañana? (Sunday)

_____

2.8.- ¿A qué día estamos? (30-04)

_____

2.9.- ¿Cuándo es tu cumpleaños? (31-01)

_____

2.10.- ¿Qué día es hoy? (27/11/2020)

_____

3.- Complete the sentences with the corresponding option.

3.1.- Hoy es 23 de _____ del 2011.

a.- lunes

b.- 02

c.- febrero

3.2.- Antonio se graduó en _____.

a.- 18

b.- mañana

c.- 1995

3.3.- P: ¿Cuándo cumples años? R: El __ de marzo.

a.- 1978

b.- 26

c.- vigésimo

3.4.- Mi aniversario de bodas es en _____.

a.- junio

b.- 1996

c.- 13

3.5.- P: ¿A qué fecha estamos? R: Estamos _ 29 de noviembre.

a.- de

b.- a

c.- en

3.6.- Colón descubrió América el 12 de octubre __ 1492.

a.- a

b.- en

c.- de

3.7.- El año comienza el _____ de enero.

a.- uno

b.- primero

c.- lunes

3.8.- Mañana es 28 de ____.

a.- mayo

b.- 2020

c.- 12

3.9.- P: ¿Qué _____ es hoy? R: Hoy es 29.

a.- mes

b.- fecha

c.- semana

3.10.- Ayer fue __ de abril.

a.- 2020

b.- 14

c.- 32

4.- Correctly organize the following sentences.

4.1.- 1998 de enero 15 de

_____

4.2.- Hoy es marzo del 25 2019 de.

_____

4.3.- Mi madre nació 1935 el abril de 11 de.

_____

4.4.- diciembre de 1963 de 28

_____

4.5.- 11-1995-20

_____

4.6.- 17 de 2016 del agosto

_____

4.7.- Mi hermano cumple años el enero de 31.

_____

4.8.- octubre de 2018 del martes, 23

_____

4.9.- 2016-28-9

4.10.- Mañana es julio de 5.

5.- Underline the grammatical error in each of these sentences.

    5.1.- Hoy es 24 de Noviembre de 2014.

    5.2.- Estamos en 26 de mayo.

    5.3.- El aniversario de la empresa es el 29 en febrero.

    5.4.- La fecha para el evento es 15 del junio del 2021.

    5.5.- ¿Qué día a hoy?

    5.6.- Ellos se van de 25 de agosto.

    5.7.- El juego fue el 19 de septiembre del 2.018.

    5.8.- Las clases se iniciarán el uno de octubre.

    5.9.- Las vacaciones son del agosto.

    5.10.- El último congreso fue el 22 de abril en 2018.

Translations:

Translate the following sentences into English:

1.- El hotel se inauguró el 21 de agosto del 2010.

_____

2.- Compramos nuestra casa nueva el 5 de mayo del 2013.

_____

3.- Mi mejor amigo cumple años el primero de marzo.

_____

4.- Nuestro viaje comenzó el 21 de septiembre del 1995.

_____

5.- Las elecciones se celebrarán el 6 de diciembre.

_____

6.- La boda se celebró el 29 de junio de 1996.

_____

7.- ¿Qué día es hoy? Hoy es 29 de octubre.

_____

8.- ¿A qué fecha estamos? Estamos a 16 de junio.

_____

9.- La mejor noche del año es la del 24 de diciembre.

_____

10.- El trabajo se concluyó el 30 de noviembre del 2019.

_____

Story:

Cuando empecé a trabajar en una oficina nueva el año pasado, el 15 de enero de 2019, mi vida cambió. El trabajo es muy bueno, y todos mis compañeros son **amistosos**: incluso mi **jefe** es simpático. Pronto descubrí que en la oficina había muchas **tradiciones**. Todos los lunes, uno de nosotros lleva **café** y **dulces** para que empecemos la semana muy animados. Y todos los viernes 13 vemos una **película** de terror en la oficina. En Navidad, el 25 de diciembre, no trabajamos, y el primero de enero de 2020 todos nos deseamos un feliz año nuevo.

En uno de los **pasillos** de la oficina hay un gran **calendario**. Ahí están anotadas todas las fechas especiales, incluyendo los **cumpleaños** de todos los que trabajamos en la oficina. El 19 de enero es el **cumpleaños** de Miguel, y está escrito con verde porque es su color favorito. El 25 de marzo es el **cumpleaños** de Alejandra, y está marcado con un dibujo de su **flor** favorita. El 2 de junio es el **cumpleaños** de nuestro **jefe**, y lo marcamos con un corazón y un signo de dólar. Mi **cumpleaños** es el 31 de octubre, y ese día también es Halloween, así que lo marcamos con un dibujo de un pequeño fantasma con un sombrero de fiesta. Es la mejor oficina del mundo.

Vocabulary:

1. Amistoso – Friendly
2. Jefe – Boss
3. Tradiciones – Traditions
4. Café – Coffee
5. Dulces – Sweets
6. Película – Movie
7. Pasillo – Hallway
8. Calendario – Calendar
9. Cumpleaños – Birthdays
10. Flor – Flower

Translated Story:

When I started working in a new office last year, on January 15 of 2019, my life changed. The job is very good, and all my colleagues are **friendly**: even my **boss** is nice. I soon discovered that there were many **traditions** in the office. Every Monday, one of us brings **coffee** and **sweets** so we start the week feeling very lively. And every Friday the 13th we watch a horror **movie** at the office. At Christmas, on December 25, we did not work, and on January 1st of 2020 we all wished each other a happy new year.

In one of the **hallways** of the office there is a large **calendar**. All the special dates are listed there, including the **birthdays** of all of us who work in the office. Miguel's **birthday** is January 19 and it is written in green because it is his favorite color. On March 25th it's Alejandra's **birthday**, and it is marked with a drawing of her favorite **flower**. Our **boss' birthday** is on June 2, and we marked it with a heart and a dollar sign. My **birthday** is on October 31st, and that day is also Halloween, so we marked it with a picture of a little ghost with a party hat. It is the best office in the world.

Questions:

1. ¿Cuándo empezó a trabajar en la oficina? _____

   When did he start to work in the office?

2. ¿Dónde hay tradiciones? _____

   Where are there traditions?

3. ¿Qué día no trabajan en la oficina? _____

   What day don't they work in the office?

4. ¿Dónde está el calendario? _____

   Where is the calendar?

5. ¿Cuál es el color favorito de Miguel? _____

   What is Miguel's favorite color?

6. ¿Cuándo cumple años el jefe? _____

   When is the boss' birthday?

Answers:

1.1.- 28 de diciembre de 1963

1.2.- 29 de junio de 1996

1.3.- 16 de junio de 1998

1.4.- 13 de agosto del 2013

1.5.- 4 de enero del 2016

1.6.- lunes, 25 de septiembre del 2002

1.7.- 21 de mayo del 2005

1.8.- jueves, 24 de febrero de 1994

1.9.- 11 de abril de 1935

1.10.- 31 de enero del 2000

2.1.- Hoy es 19 de febrero.

2.2.- Estamos a 24 de septiembre.

2.3.- Es martes.

2.4.- Sale el 12 de octubre del 2021.

2.5.- Estamos a lunes, 15.

2.6.- Hoy es 17 de noviembre.

2.7.- Mañana es domingo.

2.8.- Estamos a 30 de abril.

2.9.- Mi cumpleaños es el 31 de enero.

2.10.- Hoy es 27 de noviembre del 2020.

3.1.- c

3.2.- c

3.3.- b

3.4.- a

3.5.- b

3.6.- c

3.7.- b

3.8.- a

3.9.- b

3.10.- b

4.1.- 15 de enero de 1998

4.2.- Hoy es 25 de marzo del 2019

4.3.- Mi madre nació el 11 de abril de 1935

4.4.- 28 de diciembre de 1963

4.5.- 20-11-1995

4.6.- 17 de agosto del 2016

4.7.- Mi hermano cumple años el 31 de enero

4.8.- martes, 23 de octubre del 2018

4.9.- 28-9-2016

4.10.- Mañana es 5 de julio

5.1.- Hoy es 24 de noviembre de 2014 (noviembre)

5.2.- Estamos en 26 de mayo (a)

5.3.- El aniversario de la empresa es el 29 en febrero (de)

5.4.- La fecha para el evento es 15 del junio del 2021 (de)

5.5.- ¿Qué día a hoy? (es)

5.6.- Ellos se van de 25 de agosto (el)

5.7.- El juego fue el 19 de septiembre del 2.018 (2018)

5.8.- Las clases se iniciarán el uno de octubre (primero)

5.9.- Las vacaciones son del agosto (en)

5.10.- El último congreso fue el 22 de abril en 2018 (del)

Translations:

1.- The hotel was inaugurated on **August 21, 2010.**

2.- We bought our new house on **May 5, 2013**.

3.- My best friend's birthday is on the **first of March**.

4.- Our journey began on **September 21, 1995**.

5.- The elections will be held on **December 6**.

6.- The wedding took place on **June 29, 1996.**

7.- What day is today? Today **is October 29**.

8.- What date are we? We are **June 16.**

9. The best night of the year is that of **December 24**.

10.- The work was concluded on **November 30, 2019.**

Story:

1. El 15 de enero de 2019. – 15th of January, 2019.

2. En la oficina. – In the office.

3. El 25 de diciembre. –25th of December.

4. En el pasillo. – In the hallway.

5. Verde. – Green.

6. El 2 de junio. – 2nd June.

Chapter 9
QUESTIONS

There is an old saying in Spanish that says: "*By asking, you can get to Rome*" and when you finish this chapter, you will be able to get to Spain and Latin America, because now we will learn how to ask questions in Spanish properly.

You can review **greetings** (chapter 1) and **courtesy rules** (chapter 2) that involve questions such as *How are you?* and review **how to ask the date and time** (chapters 7 and 8), as this will help you in this topic.

Questions in Spanish are **always** framed between question marks; an inverted one for opening (¿) and a normal one for closing (?). The words we use to ask questions are called **interrogative pronouns** and they **all have an accent** (´) on a vowel. When they are used to answer a question, they do not have the **accent**, as seen here:

¿Qué? = What?
Asking about a subject or an action.

Examples:

1. - P: ¿Qué vas a hacer hoy? R: Estudiar.
    - Q: What are you going to do today? A: Study.

2. - ¿Qué es eso?
    - What is that?

3. - ¿Qué hay en la caja?
    - What is in the box?

¿Quién? O ¿Quiénes? = Who?

Asking about a person.

Examples:

1. - P: ¿Quién es tu amiga? R: Ella es Ana.

    - Q: Who is your friend? A: This is Ana.

2. - ¿Con quién vienes a cenar?

    - Who are you coming to dinner with?

3. - ¿Quién está en la puerta?

    - Who is at the door?

¿Dónde? O ¿Adónde? = Where?

Asking about a place or position. Adónde refers to a destination.

Examples:

1. - ¿Dónde naciste?

    - Where were you born?

2. - P: ¿Dónde está mi maleta? R: En la silla.

    - Q: Where is my suitcase? A: On the chair.

3. - ¿Adónde vamos a comer?

    - Where are we going to eat?

¿Cómo? = How?

Asking about how to get somewhere, or do something.

Examples:

1. - ¿Cómo llego hasta el hotel?

    - How do I get to the hotel?

2. - ¿Cómo se dice *lunch* en español?

   - How do you say *lunch* in Spanish?

3. - ¿Cómo estás?

   - How are you?

¿Cuándo? = When?

Asking about a moment in time.

   Examples:

1. - ¿Cuándo sale el avión?

   - When does the flight leave?

2. - ¿Cuándo sirven el desayuno?

   - When do you serve breakfast?

3. - P: ¿Cuándo nos vamos? R: A las 3:00pm.

   - Q: When are we leaving? A: At 3:00pm.

¿Cuántos? O ¿Cuántas? = How much? Or How many?

Asking about an amount or quantity, and they change according to the gender of the word they are referring to.

   Examples:

1. - ¿Cuánto cuesta el boleto?

   - How much is the ticket?

2. - ¿Cuántos años tienes?

   - How old are you?

135

3. - ¿Cuántas calles faltan para el museo?

   - How many streets are left to get to the museum?

¿Cuál? O ¿Cuáles? = Which? Or What?

Asking about a choice between one or more options.

Examples:

1. - ¿Cuál es tu película favorita?

   - What is your favorite movie?

2. - ¿Cuál es el bus que va al centro?

   - Which is the bus that goes to the center?

3. - ¿Cuál es la entrada?

   - Which is the entrance?

¿Por qué? = Why?

Asking for a cause or reason. It is written separately and with an accent when asking something (¿**por qué?** = *Why?*) and as a single word without an accent when used as an answer: **porque** = *Because*)

Examples:

1. - P: ¿Por qué estás triste? R: Porque mi amiga no vino.

   - Q: Why are you sad? A: Because my friend didn't come.

2. - P: ¿Por qué llegas tarde? R: Porque perdí el autobús.

   - Q: Why are you late? A: Because I missed the bus.

3. - P: ¿Por qué está cerrada la oficina? R: Porque es la hora del almuerzo.

   - Q: Why is the office closed? A: Because it's lunch time.

———————————

Exercises:

1.- Complete the question with the appropriate option from those given in the brackets.

    1.1.- ¿_____ libro compraste? R: El Quijote de la Mancha. (quién, cómo, qué)

    1.2.- ¿_____ está el lápiz? R: En la mesa. (dónde, cuál, qué)

    1.3.- ¿_____ usas guantes? R: Porque tengo frío (dónde, quién, por qué)

    1.4.- ¿_____ sigue tu tía? R: Está bien, gracias. (cuál, quién, cómo)

    1.5.- ¿_____ camisas compraste? R: Compré tres camisas. (dónde, cuántas, quién)

    1.6- ¿_____ vienes a mi casa? R: Voy el sábado. (cuándo, dónde, cuál)

    1.7.- ¿_____ va a la fiesta? R: Mi amiga Paola. (por qué, cómo, quién)

    1.8.- ¿_____ llego al aeropuerto? R: Toma un taxi. (por qué, quién, cómo)

    1.9.- ¿_____ queda el hotel? R: En la avenida 5. (cuándo, qué, dónde)

    1.10.- ¿_____ quieres comer? R: Una pizza. (qué, cuál, quién)

2.- Answer the following questions in English:

    2.1.- ¿Cuántos años tienes? _____

    2.2.- ¿Cuál es tu nombre? _____

    2.3.- ¿Cuándo cumples años? _____

    2.4.- ¿Cómo se llama tu papá? _____

    2.5.- ¿Te gusta la pizza? _____

    2.6.- ¿Dónde vives? _____

    2.7.- ¿Cuántos hermanos tienes? _____

    2.8.- ¿Dónde naciste? _____

    2.9.- ¿Qué día es mañana? _____

    2.10.- ¿De qué color son tus ojos? _____

3.- Choose the corresponding interrogative pronoun:

3.1.- ¿_____ vive Juan?

a.- cuándo

b.- dónde

c.- cuál

3.2.- ¿_____ hay en la bolsa?

a.- por qué

b.- qué

c.- dónde

3.3.- ¿_____ hermanos tienes?

a.- qué

b.- cuál

c.- cuántos

3.4.- ¿_____ se llama tu mamá?

a.- cómo

b.- dónde

c.- cuantos

3.5.- ¿_____ fecha es hoy?

a.- cómo

b.- qué

c.- cuantas

3.6.- ¿_____ estás tan contento?

a.- quién

b.- dónde

c.- por qué

3.7.- ¿_____ trabaja tu papá?

a.- dónde

b.- cuántos

c.- quién

3.8.- ¿_____ es tu carro?

a.- por qué

b.- quién

c.- cuál

3.9.- ¿_____ es tu cantante favorito?

a.- dónde

b.- cuándo

c.- quién

3.10.- ¿_____ es la reunión?

a.- cuándo

b.- quién

c.- cuántas

4.- Select the correct question for each of the following answers:

4.1.- Yo tengo 22 años.

a.- ¿Cuál es tu nombre?

b.- ¿Quién viene contigo?

c.- ¿Cuántos años tienes?

4.2.- Mi novia se llama Judith.

a.- ¿Cuantos hermanos tiene tú novia?

b.- ¿Cómo se llama tu novia?

c.- ¿Qué vamos a comer?

4.3.- Mi hija vive en Suecia.

a.- ¿Dónde vive tu hija?

b.- ¿Cómo se llama tu hija?

c.- ¿En qué trabaja tu hija?

4.4.- Yo quiero mi café con leche y azúcar.

a.- ¿Cuánto cuesta el café?

b.- ¿Dónde venden café?

c.- ¿Cómo quieres tu café?

4.5.- Nuestro tren sale a las tres y quince.

a.- ¿Cuál es nuestro tren?

b.- ¿Cuándo sale nuestro tren?

c.- ¿De dónde sale nuestro tren?

4.6.- El auto de Antonio es negro.

a.- ¿Cuántos autos tiene Antonio?

b.- ¿Dónde está el auto de Antonio?

c.- ¿De qué color es el auto de Antonio?

4.7.- Mi actor favorito es Al Pacino.

a.- ¿Quién es tu actor favorito?

b.- ¿Quién es tu cantante favorito?

c.- ¿Cuál es tu película favorita?

4.8.- Porque no me gusta ese color.

a.- ¿Por qué no compras la camisa verde?

b.- ¿Cuál es tu color favorito?

c.- ¿De qué color es esa camisa?

4.9.- Llevo mi laptop y el cargador.

a.- ¿Cuántos bolsos tienes?

b.- ¿De qué color es tu bolso?

c.- ¿Qué llevas en tu bolso?

4.10.- Mañana es domingo.

a.- ¿Qué día es hoy?

b.- ¿Qué día es mañana?

c.- ¿Qué día fue ayer?

5.- Select the correct answer from the column on the right.

5.1.- ¿De qué color son sus ojos?	A.- Son las dos y cinco.
5.2.- ¿Adónde vamos a estudiar?	B.- Yo cumplo años en junio.
5.3.- ¿Cómo se llama tu mamá?	C.- Voy a comprar seis lápices.
5.4.- ¿Quién te regaló esa bufanda?	D.- Sus ojos son verdes.
5.5.- ¿Qué fecha es hoy?	E.- Estoy bien, gracias.
5.6.- ¿Qué hora es?	F.- Vamos a la biblioteca.
5.7.- ¿Cuántos lápices vas a comprar?	G. Quiero una hamburguesa.
5.8.- ¿Cómo estás?	H.- Mi mamá se llama Ana.
5.9.- ¿Qué quieres comer?	I.- Me la regaló mi papá.
5.10.- ¿En qué mes cumples años?	J.- Hoy es 30 de noviembre.

Translations:

Translate the following sentences into English:

1.- ¿Cuál es tu color favorito?

_____

2.- ¿Cuándo cumples años?

_____

3.- ¿Adónde vas en vacaciones?

_____

4.- ¿Qué te gusta comer?

_____

5.- ¿Cuánto cuesta el boleto de avión?

_____

6.- ¿Qué tienes en tu bolso?

_____

7.- ¿Cómo se llama tu perro?

_____

8.- ¿Por qué no fuiste a clase ayer?

_____

9.- ¿Dónde están las llaves del auto?

_____

10.- ¿Quiénes viven contigo?

_____

Story:

La primera vez que fui con mi familia a Madrid, terminamos **perdidos**. ¿Cómo? es la **pregunta** de todos. Accidentalmente, respondemos. ¿Por qué? nos preguntan también. Porque no conocíamos la **ciudad**, y funciona de forma **diferente** a cualquier otro lugar donde hemos estado. ¿Quiénes? nos han preguntado también. Nuestra **respuesta** es que normalmente nos perdíamos todos juntos, pero un par de veces nos perdimos solos y los demás tuvieron que buscarnos. ¿Dónde? preguntan algunos, pero a ellos les respondemos lo **obvio**, ¡no sabíamos dónde estábamos!

Nos perdimos, por ejemplo, cuando alguien nos recomendó que tomáramos un autobús hasta el hotel. ¿Cuál autobús? preguntamos, pero antes de **escuchar** la respuesta subimos al primer bus que encontramos, el cual iba en la **dirección** opuesta. Así que tuvimos que caminar y preguntarle a un **policía** ¿Cómo llegar hasta el hotel? El **policía** nos respondió ¿Qué hotel? Y al parecer pronunciamos mal el nombre, porque ¡llegamos a un hotel totalmente **diferente**! Tuvimos que cambiar de hotel, y comprar un **mapa**.

Vocabulary:

1. Perdimos – Lost	6. Obvio – Obvious
2. Pregunta – Question	7. Escuchar – Hearing
3. Ciudad – City	8. Dirección – Direction
4. Diferente – Different	9. Policía – Policeman
5. Respuesta – Answer	10. Mapa – Map

Translated Story:

The first time I went with my family to Madrid, we ended up **lost**. How? is everyone's **question**. Accidentally, we respond. Why? they also ask us. Because we didn't know the **city**, and it works in a **different** way than anywhere else we've been. Who? they have asked us too. Our **answer** is that normally we all got lost together, but a couple of times we got lost alone and the others had to find us. Where? some ask, but we answer them with the **obvious**; we didn't know where we were!

We got lost, for example, when someone recommended that we take a bus to the hotel. Which bus? we asked, but before **hearing** the answer we got on the first bus we found, which was going in the opposite **direction**. So, we had to walk and ask a **policeman** how to get to the hotel? The **policeman** answered us: What hotel? And apparently, we mispronounced the name, because we arrived at a totally **different** hotel! We had to change hotels, and buy a **map**.

Questions:

1. ¿En cuál ciudad nos perdimos? _____

   Which city did we get lost in?

2. ¿Cómo nos perdimos? _____

   How did we get lost?

3. ¿Cómo funcionaba la ciudad? _____

   How did the city work?

4. ¿En qué tipo de carro viajamos? _____

   What kind of car did we travel in?

5. ¿A quién le preguntamos cómo llegar al hotel? _____

   Who did we ask how to get to the hotel?

6. ¿Qué compramos al final? _____

   What did we buy in the end?

Answers:

1.1.- Qué - what

1.2.- Dónde - where

1.3.- Por qué - why

1.4.- Cómo - how

1.5.- Cuántas – how many

1.6.- Cuándo - when

1.7.- Quién - who

1.8.- Cómo - how

1.9.- Dónde - where

1.10.- Qué - what

2.1.- I am __ years old.

2.2.- My name is _____.

2.3.- My birthday is on __ of _____.

2.4.- My father's name is _____.

2.5.- ___ I like pizza (or) ____I don't like pizza.

2.6.- I live in _____.

2.7.- I have __ siblings. (or) I have no siblings.

2.8.- I was born in _____.

2.9.- Tomorrow is _____.

2.10.- My eyes are _____.

3.1.- b

3.2.- b

3.3.- c

3.4.- a

3.5.- b

3.6.- c

3.7.- a

3.8.- c

3.9.- c

3.10.- a

4.1.- c

4.2.- b

4.3.- a

4.4.- c

4.5.- b

4.6.- c

4.7.- a

4.8.- a

4.9.- c

4.10.- b

5.1.- D

5.2.- F

5.3.- H

5.4.- I

5.5.- J

5.6.- A

5.7.- C

5.8.- E

5.9.- G

5.10.- B

Translations:

1.- What is your favorite color?

2.- When is your birthday?

3.- Where are you going on vacation?

4.- What do you like to eat?

5.- How much does the plane ticket cost?

6.- What do you have in your bag?

7.- What is your dog's name?

8.- Why didn't you go to class yesterday?

9.- Where are the car keys?

10.- Who lives with you?

Story:

1. En Madrid. – In Madrid.

2. Accidentalmente. – Accidentally.

3. De forma diferente. – In a different way.

4. En autobús. – By bus.

5. A un policía. – A policeman.

6. Un mapa. – A map.

Chapter 10

THE VERB: TO BE

In this chapter, we are going to study the verbs **ser** and **estar** that in many languages correspond to a single verb, and in English it's the verb **To Be**. We will use them to describe people, places, and objects.

Ser:

It is used to refer to facts and characteristics. Here is a table with the conjugations of the verb **ser** in three tenses:

Person	Present	Past	Future
I - Yo	Soy I am	Fui I was	Seré I will be
You - Tú	Eres You are	Fuiste You were	Serás You will be
He/She - Él/Ella	Es He/She is	Fue He/She was	Será He/She will be
We - Nosotros/Nosotras	Somos We are	Fuimos We were	Seremos We will be
You (plural) - Vosotros/Vosotras	Sois You are	Fuisteis You were	Seréis You will be
He/She (plural) - Ellos/Ellas	Son They are	Fueron They were	Serán They will be

Examples:

1. - Yo **soy** delgado.

   - I **am** thin.

2. - Tú **serás** la mejor de la clase.

   - You **will be** the best in the class.

3. - Ella **fue** mi mejor amiga.

   - She **was** my best friend.

4. - Nosotros **somos** latinoamericanos.

   - We **are** Latin Americans.

5. - Vosotros **seréis** los invitados de honor.

   - You **will be** the guests of honor.

6. - Ellos **fueron** castigados.

   - They **were** punished.

<u>Estar</u>:

It is used to describe perceptions, states, locations and opinions. Here is a table with the conjugations of the verb **estar**:

Person	Present	Past	Future
I - Yo	Estoy I am	Estuve I was	Estaré I will be
You - Tú	Estás You are	Estuviste You were	Estarás You will be
He/She - Él/Ella	Está He/She is	Estuvo He/She was	Estará He/She will be
We - Nosotros/Nosotras	Estamos We are	Estuvimos We were	Estaremos We will be
You (plural) - Vosotros/Vosotras	Estáis You are	Estuvisteis You were	Estaréis You will be
He/She (plural) - Ellos/Ellas	Están They are	Estuvieron They were	Estarán They will be

<u>Examples:</u>

1. - Yo **estoy** contento con el juego.
   - I **am** happy with the game.

2. - ¿Tú **estuviste** en la fiesta?
   - **Were** you at the party?

3. - Él **estará** feliz por el regalo.
   - He **will be** happy about the gift.

4. - Nosotros **estaremos** en tu casa para Navidad.
   - We **will be** in your home for Christmas

5. - Vosotros **estuvisteis** muy bien en las pruebas.
   - You **were** very good in the tests.

6. - Ellas **están** contentas con los resultados.
   - They **are** happy with the results.

———————

Exercises:

1.- Underline the verbs **ser** or **estar** in the following sentences.

      1.1.- Ella está escuchando música.

      1.2.- Nosotros estamos contentos.

      1.3.- Ellos son muy divertidos.

      1.4.- Yo soy muy delgado.

      1.5.- Ana es muy inteligente.

      1.6.- Juan y Alejandro están en Buenos Aires.

      1.7.- Ya son las cuatro de la tarde.

      1.8.- Daniela está vestida de morado.

      1.9.- Hoy es viernes.

      1.10.- Judith es muy bonita.

2.- Choose the correct verb, **ser** or **estar**, from the options in brackets.

      2.1.- Mi esposa _____ muy bonita. (somos, es)

      2.2.- Ellos _____ los profesores. (están, serán)

      2.3.- Nosotros _____ en Paris hace dos años. (estuvimos, fueron)

      2.4.- Antonio _____ el jefe de la oficina. (es, son)

      2.5.- Vosotras _____ mis invitadas. (soy, seréis)

      2.6.- Yo _____ enojado contigo. (estoy, soy)

      2.7.- Ayer _____ sábado. (fue, será)

      2.8.- El azul _____ un color bonito. (son, es)

      2.9.- La fiesta _____ el próximo mes. (están, será)

      2.10.- Daniela _____ durmiendo. (es, está)

3.- Select the correct verb, **ser** or **estar**, from the right column.

      3.1.- Yo ___ malo en matemática.   A.- es

      3.2.- Gabriela y María ____ enfermas ayer.   B.- son

3.3.- Nosotros _____ elegidos.　　　　C.- estuvo

3.4.- Vosotros ____ los dos mejores.　　D.- están

3.5.- Mi hermana __ morena.　　　　　　E.- estás

3.6.- Ellos _____ en el trabajo ahora.　　F.- fuimos

3.7.- Tú ____ una gran amiga.　　　　　G.- soy

3.8.- ___ las tres y cinco minutos.　　　H.- sois

3.9.- ¿Tú _____ enfadada?　　　　　　　I.- eres

3.10.- El ratón _____ en la cocina.　　J.- estuvieron

4.- Select the correct **to be** verb.

4.1.- Yo _____ de Venezuela.

a.- somos

b.- es

c.- soy

4.2.- Ana _____ en la escuela.

a.- está

b.- es

c.- fuimos

4.3.- Ellas _____ en una fiesta ayer.

a.- están

b.- estuvieron

c.- estarán

4.4.- Nosotros _____ los hermanos de ella.

a.- somos

b.- estamos

c.- es

153

4.5.- Ella _____ vestida de rojo ahora.

a.- será

b.- estuvo

c.- está

4.6.- Mi novia _____ médico.

a.- está

b.- es

c.- soy

4.7.- Vosotros _____ los únicos en la casa.

a.- están

b.- somos

c.- seréis

4.8.- Jorge y Ramón _____ hermanos.

a.- están

b.- es

c.- son

4.9.- La reunión _____ a la una de la tarde.

a.- estuvo

b.- es

c.- estaré

4.10.- Tú _____ la mejor en tu trabajo.

a.- serás

b.- soy

c.- estamos

5.- Write the correct conjugation of **ser** or **estar**, depending on the person and tense.

    5.1.- Presente del verbo **ser**: Yo _____.

    5.2.- Futuro del verbo **estar**: Nosotros _____.

    5.3.- Pasado del verbo **estar**: Ellas _____.

    5.4.- Futuro del verbo **ser**: Tú _____.

    5.5.- Pasado del verbo **ser**: Vosotros _____.

    5.6.- Presente del verbo **estar**: Él _____.

    5.7.- Futuro del verbo **ser**: Ellos _____.

    5.8.- Pasado del verbo **estar**: Yo _____.

    5.9.- Presente del verbo **ser**: Nosotras _____.

    5.10.- Futuro del verbo **estar**: Vosotras _____.

Translations:

Translate the following sentences into English:

1.- Ella **estuvo** bailando toda la noche.

_____

2.- Nosotros **estamos** almorzando.

_____

3.- Ellos **están** en Madrid.

_____

4.- Judith **es** una buena doctora.

_____

5.- Vosotros **seréis** el futuro del país.

_____

6.- Yo **estoy** cansado de trabajar.

_____

7.- Daniela **es** una jefa muy exigente.

_____

8.- Tú **estarás** hablando español muy pronto.

_____

9.- Los niños **están** jugando en el parque.

_____

10.- El libro **está** en la mesa.

_____

Story:

En la ciudad hay una **guardería** llamada "Estrellas del **Futuro**." El lugar está en la calle principal, y fue hogar de muchos **niños**. Ahí van muchos **niños** pequeños a aprender cosas nuevas y jugar juntos. En el patio de juegos hay muchos **juguetes**, y entre ellos hay uno que es especial, el favorito de Taylor, una niña que también es muy especial. Se trata de una **bola** de cristal, que en realidad es de plástico. A Taylor le gusta jugar a que puede ver el presente, pasado o el **futuro** en su **bola** de cristal de **juguete**.

A la profesora suele decirle, "Puedo ver que su perro, Toby está durmiendo en su **cama**." A su **mejor** amiga le dice, "Puede ver que algún día serás un astronauta, e irás a la luna." A otro de sus amigos, le dijo riendo, "Veo en mi **bola** de cristal que tú eras un bebé muy **feo**." Taylor también usaba su **poder** para el bien. Cuando la profesora acusó a sus amigos de **romper** un **juguete**, Taylor dijo "Aquí veo que ellos no fueron." Y cuando uno de sus amigos le preguntó quiénes eran los **mejores** amigos del mundo, Taylor dijo "¡Aquí veo que todos nosotros somos los **mejores** amigos del mundo!"

Vocabulary:

1. Guardería – Kindergarten
2. Futuro – Future
3. Niños – Children
4. Juguetes – Toys
5. Bola – Ball
6. Cama – Bed
7. Mejor – Best
8. Feo – Ugly
9. Poder – Power
10. Romper – Break

Translated Story:

In the city there is a **kindergarten** called "Stars of the **Future**." The place is on the main street, and it was home to many **children**. Many young **children** go there to learn new things and play together. In the playground, there are many **toys**, and among them, there is one that is special, Taylor's favorite, a girl who is also very special. It is a crystal **ball**, which is actually made of plastic. Taylor likes to pretend that she can see the present, the past, or the **future** in her **toy** crystal ball.

To the teacher, she often says, "I can see your dog, Toby is sleeping in his **bed**." To her **best** friend she says, "I can see that one day you will be an astronaut, and you will go to the moon." To another of her friends, she laughed, "I see in my crystal **ball** that you were a very ugly **baby**." Taylor also used her **power** for good. When the teacher accused her friends of **breaking** a **toy**, Taylor said "I see here that they weren't." And when one of her friends asked her who the **best** friends in the world were, Taylor said "Here I see that we are all the **best** friends in the world!"

Questions:

1. ¿Cómo se llama la guardería? _____

   What do they call the kindergarten?

2. ¿Cómo se llama la niña especial? _____

   What do they call the special girl?

3. ¿Cuál era su juguete favorito? _____

   What was her favorite toy?

4. ¿Dónde estaba Toby? _____

   Where was Toby?

5. ¿Adónde va a ir la mejor amiga? _____

   Where is the best friend going to go?

6. ¿Cómo era el otro amigo de bebé? _____

   How was the other friend as a baby?

Answers:

1.1.- está - is

1.2.- estamos - we are

1.3.- son - are

1.4.- soy - I am

1.5.- es - is

1.6.- están - are

1.7.- son - are

1.8.- está - is

1.9.- es - is

1.10.- es - is

2.1.- es - is

2.2.- serán - will be

2.3.- estuvimos - we were

2.4.- es - is

2.5.- seréis - you will be

2.6.- estoy - I am

2.7.- fue - was

2.8.- es - is

2.9.- será - will be

2.10.- está - is

3.1.- G

3.2.- J

3.3.- F

3.4.- H

3.5.- A

3.6.- D

3.7.- I

3.8.- B

3.9.- E

3.10.- C

4.1.- c

4.2.- a

4.3.- b

4.4.- a

4.5.- c

4.6.- b

4.7.- c

4.8.- c

4.9.- b

4.10.- a

5.1.- Yo soy - I am

5.2.- Nosotros estaremos - We will be

5.3.- Ellas estuvieron – They were

5.4.- Tú serás - You will be

5.5.- Vosotros fuisteis - You were

5.6.- Él está – He is

5.7.- Ellos serán – They will be

5.8.- Yo estuve - I was

5.9.- Nosotras somos - We are

5.10.- Vosotras estaréis - You will be

Translations:

1.- She **was** dancing all night.

2.- We **are** having lunch.

3.- They **are** in Madrid.

4.- Judith **is** a good Doctor.

5.- You **will be** the future of the country.

6.- I **am** tired of working.

7.- Daniela **is** a very demanding boss.

8.- You will **be** speaking Spanish very soon.

9.- The children **are** playing in the park.

10.- The book **is** on the table.

Story:

1. Estrellas del Futuro. – Stars of the Future.

2. Taylor. – Taylor.

3. Una bola de cristal. – A crystal ball.

4. En su cama. – In his bed.

5. A la luna. – To the moon.

6. Feo. – Ugly.

Chapter 11
ADJECTIVES

Adjectives describe the characteristics of a noun. They are words that express the qualities of a noun and have to agree with the gender (masculine or feminine) and number (singular or plural) of the noun.

We are now going to look at different types of adjectives.

Types of adjective:

1.- **Qualifying Adjectives**: designate a quality specific to the noun or explain some of its properties.

Examples:

1. - El libro **pequeño**.
   - The **little** book.
2. - Las casas **verdes**.
   - The **green** houses.
3. - Los hombres **gordos**.
   - The **fat** men.

2.- **Demonstrative Adjectives**: express a relationship of proximity or distance with respect to the noun. These are as follows:

	This	That	That (when the noun is further away)
Masculine	Este	Ese	Aquel
Feminine	Esta	Esa	Aquella

Examples:

1. - **Este** es mi lápiz.
   - **This** is my pencil.

2. - **Aquel** barco.

    - **That** boat.

3. - **Ese** es un globo.

    - **That** is a balloon.

3.- **Possessive Adjectives**: indicate ownership or possession of the noun. These adjectives correspond to:

	Singular noun		Plural nouns	
	Masculine	**Feminine**	**Masculine**	**Feminine**
my	mi	mi	mis	mis
mine	mío	mía	míos	mías
your	tu	tu	tus	tus
yours	tuyo	tuya	tuyos	tuyas
his / her / its / their / your (ustedes)	su	su	sus	sus
his / her / theirs / yours (ustedes)	suyo	suya	suyos	suyas
our / ours	nuestro	nuestra	nuestros	nuestras
your / yours (vosotros)	vuestro	vuestra	vuestros	vuestras

Examples:

1. - **Mi** madre me ama.

    - **My** mother loves me.

2. - Ellos son **sus** amigos.

    - They are **his** friends.

3. - El libro es **nuestro**.

    - The book is **ours**.

4. - Puedes tomarlo, es **vuestro**.

    - You can take it, it is **yours**.

4.- **Numeral Adjectives**: refer to the quantity of the noun or its place in an order. They can be:

- Cardinal (one/uno, two/dos, three/tres, fifteen/quince, forty/cuarenta, etc)
- Ordinal (first/primero, second/segundo, third/tercero, last/último),
- Multiples (double/doble, triple/triple, quadruple/cuádruple)
- Partitive - fractions (half/medio, quarter/cuarto, third/tercio, fifth/quinto, etc).

Examples:

1. - Son **cinco** niños.

    - They are **five** children.

2. - Llegue **segundo** en el juego.

    - I got **second** in the game.

3. - Él gana el **doble** que ella.

    - He earns **twice** as **much** as she does.

4. - Tomé **medio** vaso de agua.

    - I had **half a** glass of water.

5.- **Indefinite adjectives**: denote generalization and do not require specific information regarding the noun. These adjectives are: some/algunos, a lot of/bastante, some/ciertos, any/cualquiera, too many/demasiados, a lot/mucho, a little/poco, none/ninguno, more/más, all/todos.

Examples:

1. - Ellos son **algunos** de mis amigos.

    - They are **some** of my friends.

2. - Tenemos **bastante** tiempo.

    - We have **a lot of** time.

3. - Ana se ríe **mucho**.

165

- Ana laughs **a lot**.

4. - Quiero **más** soda.

    - I want **more** soda.

———————

Exercises:

1.- Underline the adjective in each sentence.

       1.1.- María es bonita.

       1.2.- El carro es azul.

       1.3.- Tengo cinco cuadernos.

       1.4.- Aquella es la casa.

       1.5.- Es mí lápiz.

       1.6.- El lago es grande.

       1.7.- Queda medio pastel.

       1.8.- Judith tiene mucho calor.

       1.9.- Nuestro salón de clase.

       1.10.- El bote es feo.

2.- Specify the type of each adjective in the list below.

       2.1.- Mucho   _____

       2.2.- Negro   _____

       2.3.- Nueve   _____

       2.4.- Algunos   _____

       2.5.- Míos   _____

       2.6.- Grande   _____

       2.7.- Esas   _____

       2.8.- Triple   _____

       2.9.- Ninguno   _____

       2.10.- Pequeña   _____

3.- Select the corresponding adjective for each sentence.

       3.1.- Marta cocina comida _____.

       a.- siete

b.- verde

c.- sabrosa

3.2.- _____ montaña está lejos.

a.- Aquella

b.- Rojo

c.- Medio

3.3.- Tenemos _____ trabajo.

a.- grande

b.- mío

c.- mucho

3.4.- Se comió _____ la pizza.

a.- azul

b.- toda

c.- bonita

3.5.- Mi papá es _____.

a.- ocho

b.- grande

c.- alguno

3.6.- Vinieron _____ _____ amigos.

a.- algunos

b.- pequeño

c.- blanco

3.7.- Daniela es _____.

a.- treinta

b.- mucho

c.- bonita

3.8.- El auto es _____.

a.- algún

b.- negro

c.- doble

3.9.- David se comió _____ hamburguesa.

a.- media

b.- verde

c.- suya

3.10.- Esta es _____ guitarra.

a.- veinte

b.- todas

c.- mi

4.- Select the appropriate adjective from the right column.

4.1.- La casa es _____.	A.- mío
4.2.- _____ puede ganar.	B.- algún
4.3.- Es __ apartamento.	C.- dos
4.4.- El libro es _____.	D.- aquel
4.5.- El vaso está _____ lleno.	E.- negro
4.6.- El vendrá _____ día.	F.- Cualquiera
4.7.- Ese carro es color ____.	G.- delgadas
4.8.- Tengo ____ perros.	H.- medio
4.9.- Mis tías son muy _____.	I.- bonita
4.10.- Llegaremos a _____ puente.	J.- tu

5.- Select the correct adjective for each sentence from the options in brackets.

5.1.- Tengo _____ hambre. (mucha, cuatro)

5.2.- Esta es _____ silla. (verde, tu)

5.3.- Ana es muy_____. (alguna, buena)

5.4.- Es un auto _____. (ocho, blanco)

5.5.- Antonio es_____. (doble, alto)

5.6.- El lapicero es_____. (azul, todos)

5.7.- José tiene _____ gatos. (tres, delgado)

5.8.- Ese es _____ sombrero. (bueno, su)

5.9.- _____ árbol es un manzano. (Aquel, Mucho)

5.10.- El perro es _____. (cualquiera, nuestro)

Translations:

Translate the following sentences into English:

1.- El domingo es un día **bonito**.

_____

2.- Me gusta **mucho** la pizza.

_____

3.- Mi hermano es **delgado**.

_____

4.- El niño tiene **varias** pelotas.

_____

5.- Hay que ver el vaso **medio** lleno.

_____

6.- Eres el **primero** de la lista.

_____

7.- Toma **tu** cuaderno.

_____

8.- No me gustan los pantalones **marrones**.

_____

9.- Esas son **nuestras** bicicletas.

_____

10.- **Algunos** amigos están en casa.

_____

Story:

    ¿Han escuchado **hablar** de una cita a ciegas? Se trata de una **primera** cita, con una persona especial, que hasta ese momento no conoces. Ahora, ¿han escuchado **hablar** de una entrevista de trabajo a ciegas? Eso no es algo muy **común**. Es algo que tan sólo he escuchado que le pasó a mi **amiga** Paola. Su **experiencia** fue muy **interesante**.

    Fue una entrevista de trabajo **sorpresa**. Ella no sabía que trabajo podían darle. Le preguntaron **cosas** muy **interesantes**. Le preguntaron si sabía **nadar**, si le gustaban las películas en blanco y negro, cuáles eran sus **alergias**. Durante la entrevista, Paola sospechó que el trabajo era en un **barco**, en un museo, o en una isla desierta.

    Al final, mi **amiga** Paola se llevó una **sorpresa** cuando le ofrecieron el trabajo de hacer entrevistas sorpresas también. Ella aceptó, por su **experiencia** se le habían ocurrido un millón de **cosas** y preguntas inesperadas para las personas que conocería.

Vocabulary:

1. Hablar – Talk
2. Primera – First
3. Común – Common
4. Experiencia – Experience
5. Interesante – Interesting
6. Sorpresa – Surprise
7. Cosas – Things
8. Nadar – Swim
9. Alergias – Allergies
10. Barco – Boat

Translated Story:

Have you heard people **talk** of a blind date? It is a **first** date, with a special person, that until that moment you have never met. Now, have you heard **talk** of a blind job interview? That is not very **common**. It's something that I've only heard has happened to my friend Paola. Her **experience** was very **interesting**.

It was a **surprise** job interview. She didn't know what job they could give her. She was asked very interesting **things**. She was asked if she knew how to **swim**, if she liked black and white movies, what were her **allergies**. During the interview, Paola suspected that the job was on a **boat**, in a museum, or on a desert island.

In the end, my friend Paola was surprised when she was offered the job of doing surprise interviews as well. She accepted; because of her experience, a million unexpected **things** and questions had occurred to her for the people she would meet.

Questions:

1. ¿Qué cosa no es común? _____

   What thing isn't common?

2. ¿Cómo fue la experiencia de Paola? _____

   How was Paola's experience?

3. ¿Cómo eran las películas? _____

   What were the movies like?

4. ¿Dónde pensó Paola que era el trabajo? _____

   Where did Paola think the job was?

5. ¿Quién se sorprendió? _____

   Who was surprised?

6. ¿Cuántas cosas se le ocurrieron a Paola? _____

   How many things occurred to Paola?

Answers:

1.1.- bonita

1.2.- azul

1.3.- cinco

1.4.- aquella

1.5.- mí

1.6.- grande

1.7.- medio

1.8.- mucho

1.9.- Nuestro

1.10.- feo

2.1.- Indefinite

2.2.- Qualifying

2.3.- Numeral

2.4.- Indefinite

2.5.- Possessive

2.6.- Qualifying

2.7.- Demonstrative

2.8.- Numeral

2.9.- Indefinite

2.10.- Qualifying

3.1.- c

3.2.- a

3.3.- c

3.4.- b

3.5.- b

3.6.- a

3.7.- c

3.8.- b

3.9.- a

3.10.- c

4.1.- I

4.2.- F

4.3.- J

4.4.- A

4.5.- H

4.6.- B

4.7.- E

4.8.- C

4.9.- G

4.10.- D

5.1.- a lot - mucha

5.2.- your - tu

5.3.- good - buena

5.4.- white - blanco

5.5.- tall - alto

5.6.- blue - azul

5.7.- three - tres

5.8.- your - su

5.9.- that - Aquel

5.10.- our - nuestro

Translations:

1.- Sunday is a **beautiful** day.

2. I like pizza a **lot**.

3.- My brother is **thin**.

4.- The child has **several** balls.

5.- You have to see the glass **half** full.

6.- You are the **first** on the list.

7.- Take **your** notebook.

8.- I don't like the **brown** pants.

9.- Those are **our** bikes.

10.- **Some** friends are at home.

Story:

1. Una entrevista de trabajo a ciegas. – A blind job interview.

2. Muy interesante. – Very interesting.

3. En blanco y negro. – Black and White.

4. Un barco, un museo, o una isla desierta – On a boat, in a museum, or on a desert island.

5. Paola. – Paola.

6. Un millón. – A million.

Chapter 12

PERSONAL PRONOUNS

Welcome to Chapter 12. You have come a long way, congratulations! Here we will concentrate on the personal pronouns in Spanish. These relate to the participants in a sentence, (people, animals, or things) but allow us to refer to these elements without naming them. That makes it possible to replace the noun, and provides information on gender (masculine or feminine) and number (singular or plural). It is a good idea to review the previous topics in Chapters 10 (**Ser y Estar**) and 11 (**Adjectives**).

Let's look at the personal pronouns in Spanish in the following table:

Person	Singular		Plural	
First	I	Yo	We (all males or mixture) We (all females)	Nosotros (masculine) Nosotras (feminine)
Second	You	Tú, Vos* Usted**	You (males or mixed) You (all females) You	Vosotros (masculine) Vosotras (feminine) Ustedes**
Third	He She	Él (masculine) Ella (femenine)	They (males or mixed) They (all females)	Ellos (masculine) Ellas (feminine)

* The pronoun Vos is used in some Latin American countries instead of Tú and Usted.

** The pronouns Usted and Ustedes are the polite, respectful or formal form of Tú and Vos.

Examples:

1. - **Yo** voy a clases.

   - **I** go to classes.

2. - **Tú** eres mi amigo. = **Vos** sois mi amigo. = **Usted** es mi amigo.

   - **You** are my friend.

3. - **Él** está feliz.

   - **He** is happy.

4. - **Ella** es maestra.

   - **She** is a teacher.

5. - **Nosotros** comemos hamburguesas.

   - **We** eat hamburgers.

6. - **Vosotros** sois los primeros en llegar. = **Ustedes** son los primeros en llegar.

   - **You** are the firsts to arrive.

7. - **Ellas** escuchan música.

   - **They** listen to music. (They are all women.)

_____

Exercises:

1.- Underline the personal pronoun in the following sentences:

       1.1.- ¿Quién es él?

       1.2.- Tú estás invitado a mi fiesta.

       1.3.- Nosotros llevaremos la comida.

       1.4.- Yo vivo en España.

       1.5.- Ellas son amigas.

       1.6.- Usted es bienvenido a mi casa.

       1.7.- Él no es el jefe.

       1.8.- Vos serás el chofer.

       1.9.- Ella es linda.

       1.10.- Nadie te amará como yo.

2.- Select the appropriate personal pronoun from the options in brackets.

       2.1.- _____ es la mejor. (él, nosotros, ella)

       2.2.- _____ soy el profesor. (yo, tú, vosotras)

       2.3.- _____ viajamos a Roma. (ella, yo, nosotros)

       2.4.- _____ es el jefe. (ellos, vosotras, usted)

       2.5.- _____ bailaron toda la noche. (tú, ellas, nosotras)

       2.6.- _____ tenías razón. (tú, nosotros, ellos)

       2.7.- _____ podéis entrar. (yo, el, vosotros)

       2.8.- _____ nos marchamos ya. (el, nosotras, ellas)

       2.9.- _____ no tengo miedo. (el, ellas, yo)

       2.10.- _____ es mi esposa. (ella, ustedes, vosotras)

3.- Write the correct personal pronoun.

       3.1.- Second person plural feminine: _____

       3.2.- Third person singular masculine: _____

       3.3.- First person plural masculine: _____

       3.4.- Third person plural feminine: _____

       3.5.- Second singular person: _____

       3.6.- First person singular: _____

       3.7.- Second person plural masculine: _____

       3.8.- Third person singular feminine: _____

       3.9.- First person plural feminine: _____

       3.10.- Third person plural masculine: _____

4.- Select the correct personal pronoun.

       4.1.- _____ vamos a la fiesta.

       a.- Yo

       b.- Nosotras

       c.- Ellas

       4.2.- _____ soy italiano.

       a.- Usted

       b.- Tú

       c.- Yo

       4.3.- _____ es mi vecino.

       a.- Ustedes

       b.- Vosotros

       c.- Él

4.4.- _____ eres mi mejor amiga.

a.- Tú

b.- Él

c.- Nosotras

4.5.- _____ irán en mi carro.

a.- Yo

b.- Nosotros

c.- Ustedes

4.6.- _____ debéis estudiar un poco más.

a.- Vosotros

b.- Ella

c.- Ellos

4.7.- _____ es muy inteligente.

a.- Nosotros

b.- Ellos

c.- Ella

4.8.- _____ tengo 22 años.

a.- Usted

b.- Yo

c.- Ellas

4.9.- _____ llegaremos el lunes.

a.- Él

b.- Nosotros

c.- Ustedes

4.10.- ¿Cómo se llama _____?

a.- Yo

b.- Ustedes

c.- Ella

5.- Select the sentence that corresponds to each personal pronoun.

5.1.- Él	A.- es mi mamá.
5.2.- Nosotros	B.- podéis todos ir en paz.
5.3.- Tú	C.- están invitados.
5.4.- Ellas	D.- iremos juntas a la playa.
5.5.- Vosotros	E.- es un amigo que vive en Madrid.
5.6.- Yo	F.- son los estudiantes de los que te hablé.
5.7.- Ustedes	G.- son mis hermanas.
5.8.- Ellos	H.- vamos unidos al congreso.
5.9.- Nosotras	I.- estoy aprendiendo español.
5.10.- Ella	J.- tienes lindos ojos.

Translations:

Translate the following sentences into English:

1.- **Ustedes** son los mejores estudiantes.

_____

2.- **Yo** cumplo 20 años en junio.

_____

3.- **Ella** va al parque los sábados.

_____

4.- **Nosotros** somos amigos desde hace 10 años.

_____

5.- **Tú** debes venir a mi casa en Nochebuena.

_____

6.- ¿Dónde vives **tú**?

_____

7.- **Él** usa una camisa verde.

_____

8.- **Ellos** son los turistas que nos visitan.

_____

9.- **Vosotros** tenéis que estar allá el 28 de diciembre.

_____

10.- ¡Hola! **Yo** soy Andrés.

_____

Story:

A todos nos gusta ver series en televisión. A los niños les gustan las series **animadas**, y a algunos adultos también. Todos vamos a **llorar** cuando vemos un drama o algo muy **romántico**. Las escenas de acción son **emocionantes** y los grandes misterios nos causan intriga. Nosotros nos dejamos llevar por la fantasía y las **aventuras**, y a veces por las historias de **fantasmas**. Pero, ¿quiénes son las personas encargadas de crear estas historias tan interesantes? Una pequeña entrevista puede revelar que a veces los **escritores** son tan interesantes como sus personajes.

"Yo soy Miguel, mi personaje favorito se llama Victoria. Ella es un **fantasma** en la serie que estoy escribiendo. **Personalmente** me gusta lo sobrenatural, e **intento** hablar con ellos, los **fantasmas**."

"Él es Andrés, trabaja en series de superhéroes y no le gustan las entrevistas. Él es **tímido**, pero todos nosotros los **escritores** lo queremos. Además, sus personajes, ellos son los favoritos del público."

Vocabulary:

1. Animadas – Animated
2. Llorar – Cry
3. Romántico – Romantic
4. Emocionantes – Exciting
5. Fantasmas – Ghost
6. Aventuras – Adventures
7. Escritores – Writers
8. Personalmente – Personally
9. Intento – I try
10. Tímido – Shy

Translated Story:

We all like to watch series on television. Children like **animated** series, and some adults too. We are all going to **cry** when we see a drama or something very **romantic**. The action scenes are **exciting** and the great mysteries intrigue us. We get carried away by fantasy and **adventures**, and sometimes by **ghost** stories. But who are the people in charge of creating these stories that are so interesting? A little interview can reveal that sometimes the **writers** are just as interesting as their characters.

"I am Miguel, my favorite character is called Victoria. She is a **ghost** in the series that I am writing. I personally like the **supernatural**, and **I try** to talk to them, the ghosts."

"He is Andrés, he works on superhero series and he doesn't like interviews. He's **shy**, but all of us **writers** love him. Besides, his characters, they are the favorites of the public."

Questions:

1. ¿Qué series les gustan a los niños? _____

   What series do children like?

2. ¿Qué hacemos al ver dramas? _____

   What do we do when we watch dramas?

3. ¿Qué escenas son emocionantes? _____

   What scenes are exciting?

4. ¿Qué es Victoria? _____

   What is Victoria?

5. ¿Qué intenta hacer Miguel? _____

   What does Miguel try to do?

6. ¿Quién es tímido? _____

   Who is shy?

Answers:

1.1.- él

1.2.- Tú

1.3.- Nosotros

1.4.- Yo

1.5.- Ellas

1.6.- Usted

1.7.- Él

1.8.- Vos

1.9.- Ella

1.10.- yo

2.1.- Ella

2.2.- Yo

2.3.- Nosotros

2.4.- Usted

2.5.- Ellas

2.6.- Tú

2.7.- Vosotros

2.8.- Nosotras

2.9.- Yo

2.10.- Ella

3.1.- Vosotras

3.2.- Él

3.3.- Nosotros

3.4.- Ellas

3.5.- Tú / vos / usted

3.6.- Yo

3.7.- Vosotros

3.8.- Ella

3.9.- Nosotras

3.10.- Ellos

4.1.- b

4.2.- c

4.3.- c

4.4.- a

4.5.- c

4.6.- a

4.7.- c

4.8.- b

4.9.- b

4.10.- c

5.1.- E

5.2.- H

5.3.- J

5.4.- G

5.5.- B

5.6.- I

5.7.- C

5.8.- F

5.9.- D

5.10.- A

Translations:

1.- **You** are the best students.

2.- **I** turn 20 in June.

3.- **She** goes to the park on Saturdays.

4.- **We** have been friends for 10 years.

5.- **You** must come to my house on Christmas Eve.

6.- Where do **you** live?

7.- **He** wears a green shirt.

8.- **They** are the tourists who visit us.

9.- **You** have to be there on December 28th.

10.- Hello! **I** am Andrés.

Story:

1. Series animadas. – Animated series.

2. Llorar. – Cry.

3. Las de acción. – Action.

4. Un fantasma. – A ghost.

5. Hablar con fantasmas. – Talk to ghosts.

6. Andrés. – Andrés.

Chapter 13
<u>VERBS</u>

We have reached Chapter 13 which deals with Verbs in Spanish. It would be a good idea to quickly review Chapters 10 **(Ser and Estar)** and 12 **(Pronouns)**.

Verbs are words that express an action, movement or state of a subject. In Spanish, verbs are conjugated, which means that their endings vary depending on the subject (I, you, he/she/it, we, you, they) and time frame (present, past, future).

Here is a list of some of the most used verbs in Spanish:

Amar – Love

Bailar – Dance

Beber – Drink

Caminar – Walk

Cantar – Sing

Cerrar – Close

Cocinar – Cook

Comer – Eat

Comprar – Buy

Correr – Run

Dormir – Sleep

Escribir – Write

Escuchar – Listen

Estudiar – Study

Gustar – Like

Hablar – Talk

Jugar – Play

Leer – Read

Oír – Listen

Pagar – Pay

Preguntar – Ask

Querer – Want

Responder – Answer

Salir – Leave

Tocar – Touch

Trabajar – Work

Usar – Use

Vender – Sell

Viajar – Travel

Vivir – Live

Now we will look at how some of these verbs conjugate in different tenses (time frames) and for different subjects (people):

Verb	Person	Present	Past	Future
AMAR **To** **Love**	**I - Yo**	amo I love	amé I loved	amaré I will love
	You - Tú	amas you love	amaste you loved	amarás you will love
	He/She - Él/Ella	ama he/she loves	amó he/she loved	amará he/she will love
	We - Nosotros/ Nosotras	amamos we love	amamos we loved	amaremos we will love
	You (plural) - Vosotros/Vosotras	amáis you love	amasteis you loved	amareis you will love
	He/She (plural) - Ellos/Ellas	aman they love	amaron they loved	amarán they will love

Verb	Person	Present	Past	Future
COMER **To Eat**	**I - Yo**	como	comí	comeré
	You – Tú	comes	comiste	comerás
	He/She - Él/Ella	come	comió	comerá
	We - Nosotros/Nosotras	comemos	comimos	comeremos
	You (plural) - **Vosotros/Vosotras**	coméis	comisteis	comeréis
	He/She (plural) - **Ellos/Ellas**	comen	comieron	comerán

Verb	Person	Present	Past	Future
ESTUDIAR **To Study**	**I - Yo**	estudio	estudié	estudiaré
	You - Tú	estudias	estudiaste	estudiaras
	He/She - Él/Ella	estudia	estudió	estudiará
	We – Nosotros/ **Nosotras**	estudiamos	estudiamos	estudiaremos
	You (plural) - **Vosotros/Vosotras**	estudiáis	estudiasteis	estudiareis
	He/She (plural) - **Ellos/Ellas**	estudian	estudiaron	estudiaran

Verb	Person	Present	Past	Future
HABLAR To Speak	I - Yo	hablo	hablé	hablaré
	You - Tú	hablas	hablaste	hablarás
	He/She - Él/Ella	habla	habló	hablará
	We - Nosotros/Nosotras	hablamos	hablamos	hablaremos
	You (plural) - Vosotros/Vosotras	habláis	hablasteis	hablareis
	He/She (plural) - Ellos/Ellas	hablan	hablaron	hablaran

Verb	Person	Present	Past	Future
JUGAR To Play	I - Yo	juego	jugué	jugaré
	You - Tú	juegas	jugaste	jugarás
	He/She - Él/Ella	juega	jugó	jugará
	We - Nosotros/Nosotras	jugamos	jugamos	jugaremos
	You (plural) - Vosotros/Vosotras	jugáis	jugasteis	jugareis
	He/She (plural) - Ellos/Ellas	juegan	jugaban	jugaran

<u>Examples</u>:

1. - Yo estudié ingeniería.

    - I studied engineering.

2. -Tú amas a tu esposo.

    - You love your husband.

3. - Él comerá espagueti.

    - He will eat spaghetti.

4. - Nosotros hablaremos mañana.

    - We will talk tomorrow.

5. - Vosotros jugáis muy bien.

    - You play very well.

6. - Ellos comieron en aquel restaurante.

    - They ate in that restaurant.

Exercises:

1.- Underline the verb in each sentence.

       1.1.- Nosotros comimos pizza.

       1.2.- Los conejos corren en el campo.

       1.3.- Tú trabajarás mañana.

       1.4.- Yo canto muy mal.

       1.5.- Hay que estudiar más.

       1.6.- Por favor escribe tu nombre.

       1.7.- Ella durmió hasta las 10:00am.

       1.8.- Vosotros jugáis muy bien al soccer.

       1.9.- Comer es un placer.

       1.10.- Es fácil hablar en español.

2.- Select the corresponding verb for each sentence.

       2.1.- Yo _____ en Madrid.

       a.- vivo

       b.- durmió

       c.- corrieron

       2.2.- Laura _____ español muy bien.

       a.- jugaran

       b.- vendieron

       c.- habla

       2.3.- Ellas ayer _____ hamburguesa.

       a.- comieron

       b.- pregunté

       c.- trabajaran

2.4.- María _____ la renta mañana.

a.- oír

b.- pagará

c.- beber

2.5.- Tú _____ la próxima semana.

a.- escribieron

b.- bailaron

c.- cocinarás

2.6.- Vosotros _____ vino en la cena.

a.- caminó

b.- beberéis

c.- miércoles

2.7.- Mañana nosotros _____ a Italia.

a.- responder

b.- viajaremos

c.- escribe

2.8.- Yo _____ a mi esposa.

a.- amo

b.- preguntaréis

c.- leer

2.9.- ¿Es fácil _____ en español?

a.- escucharon

b.- bailarían

c.- escribir

2.10.- Quiero _____ la novela "*Don Quijote De La Mancha*".

a.- saldrás

b.- leer

c.- viajaron

3.- Select the verb that is conjugated in each sentence from the options in brackets.

3.1.- Daniela juega ajedrez. (correr, vivir, jugar)

3.2.- Ellas cocinaron espagueti. (amar, cocinar, tomar)

3.3.- Yo escribí en el cuaderno. (escribir, preguntar, bailar)

3.4.- Antonio estudió ingeniería. (comer, estudiar, vivir)

3.5.- Nosotros trabajamos en casa. (caminar, salir, trabajar)

3.6.- ¿Tú te comiste todo el pan? (jugar, comer, oír)

3.7.- Vinimos caminando desde el parque. (comprar, trabajar, caminar)

3.8.- Vosotros dormiréis en esa habitación. (escribir, dormir, hablar)

3.9.- Ella baila salsa muy bien. (bailar, amar, escuchar)

3.10.- Pronto escribiré en español. (vender, pagar, escribir)

4.- Complete the sentence with the verb that is requested according to the time.

4.1.- Yo _____ dos hamburguesas. (Pasado del verbo comer)

4.2.- José _____ con ella. (Futuro del verbo hablar)

4.3.- Ellos _____ soccer. (Presente del verbo jugar)

4.4.- ¿Tú me _____ por siempre? (Futuro del verbo amar)

4.5.- Ayer yo _____ los números cn español. (Pasado del verbo estudiar)

4.6.- Nosotros _____ mañana en el parque. (Futuro del verbo jugar)

4.7.- Vosotros _____ español muy bien. (Presente del verbo hablar)

4.8.- Nosotros _____ las pizzas. (Presente del verbo amar)

4.9.- ¿Tú _____ la lección? (Pasado del verbo estudiar)

4.10.- Ella _____ conmigo mañana. (Futuro del verbo comer)

5.- Select the correct verb from the right column.

5.1.- Ella _____ una carta ayer.	A.- beber
5.2.- Nosotros _____ mañana en tu casa.	B.- canta
5.3.- Yo tengo que _____ más agua.	C.- caminó
5.4.- Ellos _____ hasta tarde hoy.	D.- dormir
5.5.- Usted _____ muy bien.	E.- caminar
5.6.- Ana _____ al trabajo.	F.- trabajarán
5.7.- El crimen no ____.	G.- escribió
5.8.- Hay que _____ 8 horas.	H.- hablas
5.9.- Es sano _____una hora al día.	I.- paga
5.10.- Tú _____ español muy bien.	J.- dormiremos

Translations:

Translate the following sentences into English:

1.- **Hablar** español es importante.

_____

2.- Tenemos que **amar** lo que hacemos.

_____

3.- Por favor **cerrar** la puerta.

_____

4.- Es divertido **comprar** regalos.

_____

5.- Me gusta **escuchar** los pájaros en la mañana.

_____

6.- **Leer** buenos libros y **tomar** buen vino.

_____

7.- Los domingos nos gusta **comer** fuera.

_____

8.- No me gusta **dormir** hasta tarde.

_____

9.- **Viajar** es un placer.

_____

10.- **Escribir** sin faltas de ortografía.

_____

Story:

Recientemente surgió un rumor de que un **grupo** de **científicos** se había reunido con un **grupo** de escritores de ciencia ficción. Los **científicos** se estaban acercando a crear una **máquina** del tiempo. Pero, hasta este momento, aún no lo habían logrado. A los **científicos** les faltaban ideas **originales** y nuevas. Por esa razón, los **científicos** hablaron con los escritores de ciencia ficción. Los escritores eran expertos en viajes en el tiempo, pero solo en sus historias. Ellos amaron la idea de **aplicar** sus teorías a la realidad.

Al principio era muy **divertido**, ver a mujeres y hombres de ciencia jugar con ideas **locas**, mientras los creadores de **mundos** de ficción juegan con ciencia de verdad por primera vez. **Juntos**, ambos **grupos** estudiaron todas las posibilidades. Ellos anunciaron que pronto hablaremos en serio de viajar en el tiempo. Pero, por ahora, parece que simplemente disfrutan estar **juntos**.

Vocabulary:

1. Recientemente – Recently
2. Grupo – Group
3. Científicos – Scientists
4. Máquina – Machine
5. Originales – Original
6. Aplicar – Applying
7. Divertido – Fun
8. Locas – Crazy
9. Mundos – Worlds
10. Juntos – Together

Translated Story:

      Λ rumor **recently** surfaced that a **group** of **scientists** had met with a **group** of science fiction writers. **Scientists** were getting close to creating a time **machine**. But, up to this point, they still hadn't achieved it. **Scientists** lacked **original** and new ideas. For that reason, the scientists spoke to science fiction writers. The writers were experts in time travel, but only in their stories. They loved the idea of **applying** their theories to reality.

      At first it was a lot of **fun**, watching women and men of science play with **crazy** ideas, while the creators of fictional **worlds** play with real science for the first time. **Together**, both **groups** studied all the possibilities. They announced that soon we will talk seriously about time travel. But for now, it seems like they just enjoy being **together**.

Questions:

1. ¿Quiénes se reunieron? _____

   Who met up?

2. ¿Qué querían crear los científicos? _____

   What did the scientists want to create?

3. ¿Qué les faltaba a los científicos? _____

   What did the scientists lack?

4. ¿Quiénes eran expertos en viajes en el tiempo? _____

   Who were experts in time travel?

5. ¿Cómo fue todo al principio? _____

   How was everything at the beginning?

6. ¿Quiénes jugaban con ideas locas? _____

   Who was playing with crazy ideas?

Answers:

1.1.- comimos

1.2.- corren

1.3.- trabajarás

1.4.- canto

1.5.- estudiar

1.6.- escribe

1.7.- durmió

1.8.- jugáis

1.9.- Comer

1.10.- hablar

2.1- a

2.2.- c

2.3.- a

2.4.- b

2.5.- c

2.6.- b

2.7.- b

2.8.- a

2.9.- c

2.10.- b

3.1.- jugar

3.2.- cocinar

3.3.- escribir

3.4.- estudiar

3.5.- trabajar

3.6.- comer

3.7.- caminar

3.8.- dormir

3.9.- bailar

3.10.- escribir

4.1.- comí

4.2.- hablará

4.3.- juegan

4.4.- amarás

4.5.- estudié

4.6.- jugaremos

4.7.- habláis

4.8.- amamos

4.9.- estudiaste

4.10.- comerá

5.1.- G

5.2.- J

5.3.- A

5.4.- F

5.5.- B

5.6.- C

5.7.- I

5.8.- D

5.9.- E

5.10.- H

Translations:

1.- **Speaking** Spanish is important.

2.- We have to **love** what we do.

3.- Please **close** the door.

4.- It's fun to **buy** gifts.

5.- I like to **listen** to the birds in the morning.

6.- **Read** good books and **drink** good wine.

7.- On Sundays we like to **eat** outside.

8.- I don't like **sleeping** late.

9.- **Traveling** is a pleasure.

10.- **Write** without spelling mistakes.

Story:

1. Científicos y escritores. – Scientists and writers.

2. Una máquina del tiempo. – A time machine.

3. Ideas originales y nuevas. – Original and new ideas.

4. Los escritores. – The writers.

5. Muy divertido. – Lots of fun.

6. Los científicos. – The scientists.

Chapter 14

<u>FUTURE</u>

In the very near future, you will be reading, writing, and speaking in Spanish, so now we are going to review everything associated with the Spanish language in the future tense. It is recommended that you revisit the topics in Chapters 10 (**Ser y Estar**) and 13 (**Verbs**) if it has been a while since you studied them.

The future is the tense which expresses that something will exist or take place at a time that is later than when the sentence is originally shared. In Spanish, there is no auxiliary verb like "Will" for the future. The ending of verbs in the future are identical, regardless of whether they end in *ar, er, or ir.* Only the following endings are added, as explained in the subsequent table, with three verbs being used as examples.

Person	Ar Verbs	Er Verbs	Ir Verbs
	Hablar (To Speak)	**Comer (To Eat)**	**Vivir (To Live)**
Yo	hablar**é**	comer**é**	Vivir**é**
Tú	hablar**ás**	comer**ás**	Vivir**ás**
Él/Ella	hablar**á**	comer**á**	Vivir**á**
Nosotros/Nosotras	hablar**emos**	comer**emos**	Vivir**emos**
Vosotros/Vosotras	hablar**éis**	comer**éis**	Vivir**éis**
Ellos/Ellas	hablar**án**	comer**án**	vivir**án**

There are some irregular verbs that not only change their ending in the future in Spanish, but also change the stem of the verb. For example, do/make, can, and say, or *hacer, poder, decir*.

Verb	Yo	Tú	Él/ Ella	Nosotros/ Nosotras	Vosotros/ Vosotras	Ellos/ Ellas
Hacer (To do/make)	haré	harás	hará	haremos	haréis	harán
Poder (To be able to)	podré	podrás	podrá	podremos	podréis	podrán
Decir (To say)	diré	dirás	dirá	diremos	diréis	dirán

Examples:

1. - Yo hablaré mañana en clase.

   - I will talk tomorrow in class.

2. - Tú comerás en mi casa el lunes.

   - You will eat in my house on Monday.

3. - Ella vivirá en Madrid por un año.

   - She will live in Madrid for a year.

4. - Nosotros haremos una fiesta.

   - We will have a party.

5. - Vosotras podréis dormir hasta tarde.

   - You will be able to sleep late.

6. - Ellos dirán lo que vieron.

   - They will say what they saw.

Exercises:

1.- Select the correct verb in the future tense from the right column.

       1.1.- Yo _____ una hamburguesa.   A.- hablarás

       1.2.- Nosotros _____ a New York.   B.- vivirá

       1.3.- Tú _____ en la reunión.   C.- Estaremos

       1.4.- Ellos _____ lo que sucedió.   D.- hará

       1.5.- Ella _____en una nueva casa.   E.- podréis

       1.6.- Vosotros no _____ iros mañana.   F.- comeré

       1.7.- José _____ la cena.   G.- pagará

       1.8.- ¿Quién _____ la cuenta?   H.- diré

       1.9.- Yo no _____ nunca tu secreto.   I.- viajaremos

       1.10.- _____ mejor este nuevo año.   J.- dirán

2.- Connect the verb in the future with the correct person.

       Verb: hablarán, hablará, hablaré, hablaréis, hablarás, hablaremos

       2.1.- Yo   _____

       2.2.- Tú   _____

       2.3.- Él   _____

       2.4.- Nosotras   _____

       2.5.- Vosotros   _____

       2.6.- Ellas   _____

       Verb: comerán, comerás, comeré, comeremos

       2.7.- Yo   _____

       2.8.- Tú   _____

       2.9.- Nosotros   _____

       2.10.- Ellos   _____

3.- Select the correct verb in the future for each subject.

3.1.- Yo _____. (cantar)

a.- cantarán

b.- cantaré

c.- cantaras

3.2.- Nosotros _____. (comer)

a.- comeremos

b.- comerán

c.- comeré

3.3.- Vosotros _____. (hablar)

a.- hablarán

b.- hablando

c.- hablaréis

3.4.- Daniel _____. (decir)

a.- dirán

b.- dirá

c.- diremos

3.5.- Luisa y Ana _____. (bailar)

a.- bailarán

b.- bailaréis

c.- bailará

3.6.- Tú _____. (vivir)

a.- vivirán

b.- viviré

c.- vivirás

3.7.- Nosotras _____. (hacer)

a.- harán

b.- haré

c.- haremos

3.8.- Yo _____. (hablar)

a.- hablarán

b.- hablaré

c.- hablaréis

3.9.- Vosotros _____. (poder)

a.- podréis

b.- podrán

c.- pueden

3.10.- Luis, María y Ramón _____. (pagar)

a.- pagaré

b.- pagarán

c.- pagará

4.- Select the correctly written sentence.

      4.1.- a.- Yo cenaremos mañana en tu casa.

      b.- Yo cenaré mañana en tu casa.

      c.- Yo cenarán mañana en tu casa.

      4.2.- a.- Nosotros irán a Madrid el próximo año.

      b.- Nosotros iremos a Madrid el próximo año.

      c.- Nosotros iréis a Madrid el próximo año.

      4.3.- a.- Mi novia tocará la guitarra en el concierto.

      b.- Mi novia tocaremos la guitarra en el concierto.

      c.- Mi novia tocarán la guitarra en el concierto.

      4.4.- a.- Ellos comeremos pizza en la noche.

      b.- Ellos comeré pizza en la noche.

      c.- Ellos comerán pizza en la noche.

      4.5.- a.- Vosotros compraréis esa casa.

      b.- Vosotros comprarán esa casa.

      c.- Vosotros compraremos esa casa.

      4.6.- a.- ¿Quién pagaremos la cuenta?

      b.- ¿Quién pagaré la cuenta?

      c.- ¿Quién pagará la cuenta?

      4.7.- a.- Mi padre trabajaré en agosto.

      b.- Mi padre trabajará en agosto.

      c.- Mi padre trabajarán en agosto.

4.8.- a.- Ana y Marcos viajarán en avión.

b.- Ana y Marcos viajaremos en avión.

c.- Ana y Marcos viajará en avión.

4.9.- a.- Tú haremos el desayuno.

b.- Tú harás el desayuno.

c.- Tú haré el desayuno.

4.10.- a.- Nosotros vivirán en ese apartamento.

b.- Nosotros viviréis en ese apartamento.

c.- Nosotros viviremos en ese apartamento.

5.- Select the correct verb from the options in brackets.

5.1.- Nosotros _____ mañana. (hablaré, hablarán, hablaremos)

5.2.- Judith _____ en la fiesta. (bailará, bailaré, bailarán)

5.3.- Tú _____ toda la noche. (estudiarán, estudiarás, estudiaremos)

5.4.- Ellos _____ en Madrid el próximo año. (viviréis, vivirán, viviré)

5.5.- Él _____ con nosotros. (comerá, comeremos, comerán)

5.6.- Yo _____ la verdad. (diremos, dirán, diré)

5.7.- Las flores _____ en primavera. (crecerán, creceréis, creceré)

5.8.- Algunos se _____ por ahí. (perderán, perderemos, perderá)

5.9.- Vosotros _____ en esa habitación. (dormirá, dormiréis, dormiremos)

5.10.- ¿Tú _____ en la cocina? (ayudaré, ayudarán, ayudarás)

Translations:

Translate the following sentences into English:

    1.- Yo te **amaré** por siempre.

_____

    2.- Nosotros **comeremos** pizza en la cena.

_____

    3.- Ella **hablará** toda la noche.

_____

    4.- Daniela **escribirá** un cuento.

_____

    5.- Antonio **trabajará** el domingo.

_____

    6.- José y Paola **vivirán** en ese apartamento.

_____

    7.- Vosotros **diréis** a todos lo que pasó.

_____

    8.- Tú **cantarás** en la fiesta.

_____

    9.- Los perros **correrán** en la plaza.

_____

    10.- Juntos **podremo**s lograrlo.

_____

Story:

El **fin** del año 1999 fue muy interesante. Al terminar el año, terminaría un siglo, y terminaría un milenio. Las personas tenían **miedo** de que con el año 2000 llegara el **fin** del mundo. En la actualidad tal vez nos parezca divertido. Pero, **seriamente**, las personas tenían **miedo**. Había muchas **teorías** locas, divertidas, e interesantes sobre lo que podría pasar.

"Las computadoras se volverán poderosas y vivirán, van a dominar el mundo," creían unas personas. "Los juguetes también," les advirtieron los hermanos **mayores** a sus **inocentes** hermanos **menores**, "ellos vivirán y serán todos **malvados**."

"Diremos adiós al **sol**, y será siempre de noche," insistieron otras personas. Los que lo creyeron, pasaron mucho tiempo en la playa, tomando el **sol**. "Así nadie dirá que estoy pálido antes de que se vaya el **sol**," decían.

"¡Podré **robar** una tienda! Porque estaremos en el fin del mundo," dijo alguien que, cuando lo atrapó la policía, descubrió que el año 2000 era un año totalmente normal.

Vocabulary:

1. Fin – End
2. Miedo – Fear
3. Seriamente – Seriously
4. Teorías – Theories
5. Mayores – Older
6. Inocentes – Innocent
7. Menores – Younger
8. Malvados – Evil
9. Sol – Sun
10. Robar – Rob

Translated Story:

The **end** of 1999 was very interesting. At the end of the year, a century would end, and a millennium would end. People had the **fear** that with the year 2000 the **end** of the world would come. Today we may find it funny. But **seriously**, people had that **fear**. There were lots of crazy, funny, and interesting **theories** about what could happen.

"Computers will become powerful and they will live; they will take over the world," some people believed. "The toys too," the **older** brothers warned their **innocent younger** brothers, "they will live and they will all be **evil**."

"We will say goodbye to the **sun**, and it will always be night," insisted other people. Those who believed it, spent a lot of time on the beach, **sun**bathing. "So no one will say that I am pale before the **sun** goes down," they said.

"I'll be able to **rob** a store! Because we will be at the end of the world," said someone who, when caught by the police, discovered that the year 2000 was a totally normal year.

Questions:

1. ¿Cómo fue el fin del año 1999? _____

   How was the end of the year 1999?

2. ¿Qué tenían las personas? _____

   What did people have?

3. ¿Cómo eran las teorías? _____

   How were the theories?

4. ¿Quiénes eran inocentes? _____

   Who were innocent?

5. ¿A qué diremos adiós? _____

   What will we say goodbye to?

6. ¿Cómo fue el año 2000? _____

   How was the year 2000?

<u>Answers:</u>

1.1.- F

1.2.- I

1.3.- A

1.4.- J

1.5.- B

1.6.- E

1.7.- D

1.8.- G

1.9.- H

1.10.- C

2.1.- hablaré

2.2.- hablarás

2.3.- hablará

2.4.- hablaremos

2.5.- hablaréis

2.6.- hablarán

2.7.- comeré

2.8.- comerás

2.9.- comeremos

2.10.- comerán

3.1.- b

3.2.- a

3.3.- c

3.4.- b

3.5.- a

3.6.- c

3.7.- c

3.8.- b

3.9.- a

3.10.- b

4.1.- b

4.2.- b

4.3.- a

4.4.- c

4.5.- a

4.6.- c

4.7.- b

4.8.- a

4.9.- b

4.10.- c

5.1.- hablaremos

5.2.- bailará

5.3.- estudiarás

5.4.- vivirán

5.5.- comerá

5.6.- diré

5.7.- crecerán

5.8.- perderán

5.9.- dormiréis

5.10.- ayudarás

Translations:

1.- I **will love** you forever.

2.- We **will eat** pizza at dinner.

3.- She **will talk** all night.

4.- Daniela **will write** a story.

5.- Antonio **will work** on Sunday.

6.- José and Paola **will live** in that apartment.

7.- You **will tell** everyone what happened.

8.- You **will sing** at the party.

9.- The dogs **will run** in the square.

10.- Together **we will be able to** achieve it.

Story:

1. Muy interesante. – Very interesting.

2. Miedo. – Fear.

3. Locas, divertidas e interesantes. – Crazy, fun and interesting.

4. Los hermanos menores. – The older brothers.

5. Al sol. – The sun.

6. Totalmente normal. – Totally normal.

Chapter 15

PAST

We have already reached Chapter 15. Congratulations! In this particular topic, we are going to learn how to read and write in the past tense in Spanish. The past tense is a bit complicated in Spanish due to the different times in which it can be written. For the purposes of this chapter, we will concentrate on the past simple tense with different verbs.

	Hablar	Estudiar	Beber	Comer	Leer	Vivir
Yo	hablé	estudié	bebí	comí	leí	viví
Tú	hablaste	estudiaste	bebiste	comiste	leíste	viviste
Él (Ella)	habló	estudió	bebió	comió	leyó	vivió
Nosotros (as)	hablamos	estudiamos	bebimos	comimos	leímos	vivimos
Vosotros (as)	hablasteis	estudiasteis	bebisteis	comisteis	leísteis	vivisteis
Ellos (Ellas)	hablaron	estudiaron	bebieron	comieron	leyeron	vivieron

Examples:

1. - Ellos lo leyeron en el periódico de ayer.

    - They read it in yesterday's newspaper.

2. - ¿Tú viviste en España?

    - Did you live in Spain?

3. - Nosotros comimos hamburguesas el sábado.

    - We ate hamburgers on Saturday.

4. - Antonio habló en el teatro.

    - Antonio spoke at the theater.

5. - Yo bebí una soda.

    - I drank a soda.

6. - ¿Vosotros estudiasteis anoche?

    - Did you study last night?

———————————

Exercises:

1.- Select the correct **past tense** of the verb in brackets for each subject.

    1.1.- Nosotros _____. (Vivir)

    a.- vivimos

    b.- viviremos

    c.- vivieron

    1.2.- Laura _____. (Hablar)

    a.- hablaron

    b.- hablé

    c.- habló

    1.3.- José y Nicolás _____. (Estudiar)

    a.- estudió

    b.- estudiaron

    c.- estudiarán

    1.4.- Tú _____. (Beber)

    a.- bebieron

    b.- beberás

    c.- bebiste

    1.5.- Vosotros _____. (Comer)

    a.- comisteis

    b.- comieron

    c.- comeréis

    1.6.- Ellas _____. (Leer)

a.- leímos

b.- leíste

c.- leyeron

1.7.- Tú y yo _____. (Hablar)

a.- hablaste

b.- hablé

c.- hablamos

1.8.- Él _____. (Comer)

a.- comió

b.- comerá

c.- comiendo

1.9.- Vosotros _____. (Leer)

a.- leyeron

b.- leísteis

c.- leerán

1.10.- Yo _____. (vivir)

a.- viviré

b.- vivió

c.- viví

2.- Select the correct option:

2.1.- a.- Ellos habló anoche.

b.- Ellos hablaron anoche.

c.- Ellos hablasteis anoche.

2.2.- a.- Tú comiste poco.

b.- Tú comerán poco.

c.- Tú comieron poco.

2.3.- a.- Yo leyeron un libro.

b.- Yo leíste un libro.

c.- Yo leí un libro.

2.4.- a.- Vosotros bebieron agua.

b.- Vosotros beberán agua.

c.- Vosotros bebisteis agua.

2.5.- a.- Judith vivió en Roma.

b.- Judith vivirán en Roma.

c.- Judith viví en Roma.

2.6.- a.- Nosotros estudié ayer.

b.- Nosotros estudiaron ayer.

c.- Nosotros estudiamos ayer.

2.7.- a.- Juan y Ana comieron en su casa.

b.- Juan y Ana comisteis en su casa.

c.- Juan y Ana comió en su casa.

2.8.- a.- Ayer beber leche.

b.- Ayer bebiendo leche.

c.- Ayer bebí leche.

2.9.- a.- ¿Tú comieron?

b.- ¿Tú comiste?

c.- ¿Tú comí?

2.10.- a.- Vosotros hablasteis la semana pasada.

b.- Vosotros hablaron la semana pasada.

c.- Vosotros hablareis la semana pasada.

3.- Write the verb in brackets in the past tense.

    3.1.- Ayer nosotros _____ (beber) Coca-Cola.

    3.2.- Yo no me _____ (comer) toda la torta.

    3.3.- Vosotros _____ (leer) muy bien.

    3.4.- Ana _____ (vivir) en mi casa.

    3.5.- Ella _____ (hablar) por 2 horas.

    3.6.- Anoche tú no _____ (estudiar).

    3.7.- Nosotros en la cena _____ (comer) pizza.

    3.8.- Juan y Alejandro _____ (vivir) en USA.

    3.9.- Daniela no _____ (comer) tomate.

    3.10.- Yo _____ (leer) el periódico.

4.- Write the verb in the past tense from the options with the correct noun.

Verbo: estudiasteis, estudió, estudiaron, estudié, estudiaste, estudiamos

    4.1.- Yo _____

    4.2.- Tú _____

    4.3.- Él/Ella _____

    4.4.- Nosotros/Nosotras _____

    4.5.- Vosotros/Vosotras _____

    4.6.- Ellos/Ellas _____

Verbo: leímos, leí, leyó, leíste

4.7.- Yo _____

4.8.- Tú _____

4.9.- Él/Ella _____

4.10.- Nosotros/Nosotras _____

5.- Select the appropriate verb from the right column.

5.1.- Yo _____ un vaso de agua.	A.- habló
5.2.- María _____ tu carta.	B.- comiste
5.3.- Ayer nosotros _____ espagueti.	C.- vivió
5.4.- Tú _____ muy bien.	D.- leí
5.5.- Ellos no _____ la lección.	E.- bebisteis
5.6.- Ella _____ un año en París.	F.- comimos
5.7.- Gabriela no _____ durante la cena.	G.- leyó
5.8.- ¿Vosotros _____ leche?	H.-bebí
5.9.- Yo no ___ tu nota.	I.- estudiaron
5.10.- Tú _____ mucha lasaña.	J.- hablaste

Translations:

Translate the following sentences into English:

    1.- El año pasado **viví** en Madrid.

    _____

    2.- Ramón **habló** de su vida con alegría.

    _____

    3.- Si tú **estudiaste** será muy fácil.

    _____

    4.- Ellos **bebieron** mucha agua.

    _____

    5.- ¿Vosotros **leísteis** el informe?

    _____

    6.- A las 3:00pm yo **comí** un pedazo de pastel.

    _____

    7.- Los que no **estudiaron** reprobaran.

    _____

    8.- Nosotros no **hablamos** en un año.

    _____

    9.- Ella **leyó** el mensaje en la pared.

    _____

    10.- Ana y Dora **vivieron** felices con su familia.

    _____

Story:

Es bien sabido en todo el mundo que, las personas, al alcanzar cierta edad **madura**, empiezan a **perder** un poco de sus capacidades mentales. Hay casos serios, que se convierten en **enfermedades** muy difíciles. Pero, también existen casos más fáciles de llevar. Muchas veces, la edad **simplemente** hace que nuestros cerebros trabajen un poco más lentos, o nos vuelve más creativos. Así que, al caminar por un parque en el que se encuentran reunidos un grupo de **ancianos**, se pueden llegar a escuchar cosas **simplemente** increíbles.

"Yo vivo solo, muy solo, y eso si es **triste**," por ejemplo, dijo uno de los abuelos que vivía en **compañía** de dos de sus hijos. "Yo preferiría vivir sola," dijo otra señora, "Por mi casa se pasean mis veintitrés nietos. Paso todo el día cambiando **pañales**." Sin embargo, el más joven de sus nietos dejó los **pañales** tres años atrás. El más creativo de los **ancianos** casi no escuchaba a los demás. Estaba muy entretenido con sus propias historias. "Cuando viví en el polo sur, los **pingüinos** y yo comíamos camarones todos los días por año. Luego, cuando bebí agua del océano antártico, los **pingüinos** me hablaron. ¡**Juro** que no estoy loco!"

Vocabulary:

1. Madura – Mature
2. Perder – Lose
3. Enfermedades – Diseases
4. Simplemente – Simply
5. Ancianos – Elderly people
6. Triste – Sad
7. Compañía – Company
8. Pañales – Diapers
9. Pingüinos – Penguins
10. Juro – Swear

Translated Story:

It is well known throughout the world that people, upon reaching a certain **mature** age, begin to **lose** a little of their mental capacities. There are serious cases, which become very difficult **diseases**. But there are also easier cases to deal with. Many times, age **simply** makes our brains work a little slower, or makes us more creative. So, when walking through a park where a group of **elderly people** are gathered, you can get to hear **simply** incredible things.

"I live alone, very lonely, and that is **sad**," for example, said one of the grandparents who lived in the **company** of two of his children. "I would prefer to live alone," said another lady, "My twenty-three grandchildren walk through my house. I spend all day changing **diapers**." However, the youngest of her grandchildren left **diapers** behind three years ago. The most creative of the **elderly people** hardly listened to others. He was very entertained with his own stories. "When I lived in the South Pole, the **penguins** and I ate shrimp every day of the year. Then when I drank water from the Antarctic Ocean, the **penguins** spoke to me. I **swear** I'm not crazy! "

Questions:

1. ¿A qué edad perdemos capacidades mentales? _____

   At what age do we lose our mental capacities?

2. ¿Cómo son las enfermedades? _____

   What are the illness like?

3. ¿Quiénes estaban en el parque? _____

   Who were in the park?

4. ¿Con cuántos hijos vive el abuelo? _____

   How many children live with the grandfather?

5. ¿Cuántos nietos tiene la señora? _____

   How many grandchildren does the lady have?

6. ¿Qué animal vive en el polo sur? _____

   What animal lives in the South Pole?

<u>Answers:</u>

1.1.- a

1.2.- c

1.3.- b

1.4.- c

1.5.- a

1.6.- c

1.7.- c

1.8.- a

1.9.- b

1.10.- c

2.1.- b

2.2.- a

2.3.- c

2.4.- c

2.5.- a

2.6.- c

2.7.- a

2.8.- c

2.9.- b

2.10.- a

3.1.- bebimos

3.2.- comí

3.3.- leísteis

3.4.- vivió

3.5.- habló

3.6.- estudiaste

3.7.- comimos

3.8.- vivieron

3.9.- comió

3.10.- leí

4.1.- estudié

4.2.- estudiaste

4.3.- estudió

4.4.- estudiamos

4.5.- estudiasteis

4.6.- estudiaron

4.7.- leí

4.8.- leíste

4.9.- leyó

4.10.- leímos

5.1.- H

5.2.- G

5.3.- F

5.4.- J

5.5.- I

5.6.- C

5.7.- A

5.8.- E

5.9.- D

5.10.- B

Translations:

1.- Last year **I lived** in Madrid.

2.- Ramón **spoke** of his life with joy.

3.- If you **studied** it will be very easy.

4.- They **drank** a lot of water.

5.- Did you **read** the report?

6.- At 3:00pm I **ate** a piece of cake.

7.- Those who did not **study** will fail.

8.- We didn't **speak** in a year.

9.- She **read** the message on the wall.

10.- Ana and Dora **lived** happily with their family.

Story:

1. A cierta edad madura. – At a certain mature age.

2. Muy difíciles. – Very difficult.

3. Un grupo de ancianos. – A group of elderly people.

4. Dos. – Two.

5. Veintitrés. – Twenty-three.

6. Pingüinos. – Penguins.

Chapter 16

NEGATIONS

There are those who say it is very difficult to learn to say "No" to some things, but it will be very easy for you, at least in Spanish, after studying this topic.

To deny something is to say it doesn't exist or hasn't occurred. Negative sentences deny what the verb expresses, deny a fact, or state that something that is happening, hasn't been completed yet.

In Spanish, the best example of negation is the adverb **no**, which must precede the verb. In negative sentences, the usual order of the elements is **subject + not + verb.**

Examples:

1. - José **no** come pescado.

    - José **does not** eat fish.

2. - Yo **no** hablo francés,

    - I **don't** speak French,

3. - Ellas **no** bailarán en la calle,

    - They will **not** dance in the street,

In Spanish, there are other adverbs that work to deny elements or actions of the sentence. These are **nadie, jamás, ningún/a, nunca, tampoco.**

Examples:

1. - **Nadie** vino a la clase.

    - **No one** came to class.

2. - **Jamás** golpearé un perro.

    - I will **never** hit a dog.

3. - **Ningún** alumno reprobó.

    - **No** student failed.

4. - Él **nunca** bebió vino.

- He **never** drank wine.

5.   - Yo **tampoco** bebí vino.

    - I **didn't** drink wine either.

Exercises:

1.- Underline the adverb of negation.

    1.1.- María no leyó el libro.

    1.2.- Vosotros nunca volveréis.

    1.3.- Jorge y Ramón jamás comieron caracoles.

    1.4.- Mi esposa tampoco habla inglés.

    1.5.- Teresa no estudia danza.

    1.6.- Nadie puede leer esto.

    1.7.- Yo no cumplo años este mes.

    1.8.- Ningún niño debe trabajar.

    1.9.- El pan no está fresco.

    1.10.- Nadie hablará en clase.

2.- Change the following sentences to their negative form, using the adverb in brackets.

    2.1.- Yo trabajo hoy. (no) _____

    2.2.- Ana baila mal. (no) _____

    2.3.- Ella ha venido aquí. (nunca) _____

    2.4.- Nosotros jugamos al básquetbol. (nunca) _____

    _____

    2.5.- vino a la reunión. (Nadie) _____

    2.6.- alumno estudió. (Ningún) _____

    2.7.- El carro está limpio. (no) _____

    2.8.- Mi hermano bebe soda. (tampoco) _____

    2.9.- Tú me olvidarás. (jamás) _____

    2.10.- me gusta el sushi. (No) _____

3.- Select the appropriate negative adverb.

3.1.- Laura _____ viaja sola.

a.- nadie

b.- nunca

3.2.- _____ vi esa película.

a.- jamás

b.- ningún

3.3.- Daniela _____ come tomate.

a.- nadie

b.- no

3.4.- _____ hace ejercicio.

a.- Ningún

b.- Nadie

3.5.- Yo _____ bebo licor.

a.- no

b.- nadie

3.6.- Ellas _____ toman el autobús.

a.- siempre

b.- nunca

3.7.- El árbol _____ tiene hojas.

a.- nadie

b.- no

3.8.- A él _____ le gusta el Rock.

a.- tampoco

b.- ningún

3.9.- ¡Aquí _____ se rinde!

a.- nosotros

b.- nadie

3.10.- Ella _____ dejará de cantar.

a.- nunca

b.- ningún

4.- Select the correct negative sentence from the options.

4.1.- a.- Yo tampoco juego al tenis.

b.- Yo nadie juego al tenis.

c.- Yo juego al tenis.

4.2.- a.- Judith no hace ejercicio.

b.- Judith siempre hace ejercicio.

c.- Judith hace ejercicio.

4.3.- a.- El edificio si es seguro.

b.- El edificio siempre es seguro.

c.- El edificio no es seguro.

4.4.- a.- Me gustó la película.

b.- No me gustó la película.

c.- Si, me gustó la película.

4.5.- a.- Nadie tomó sopa.

b.- ¿Quién se tomó la sopa?

c.- Alguien se tomó la sopa.

4.6.- a.- Daniela cumple años en octubre.

b.- Daniela si cumple años en octubre.

c.- Daniela no cumple años en octubre.

4.7.- a.- Ninguno de los gatos durmió en la caja.

b.- Tampoco de los gatos dumio en la caja.

c.- Los gatos durmieron en la caja.

4.8.- a.- La puerta está abierta.

b.- La puerta está cerrada.

c.- La puerta no está abierta.

4.9.- a.- Voy a comprar un carro.

b.- Nunca voy a comprar un carro.

c.- Si voy a comprar un carro.

4.10.- a.- Escribo con lapicero rojo.

b.- Siempre escribo con lapicero rojo.

c.- Nunca escribo con lapicero rojo.

5.- Select the appropriate negation adverb from those found in the brackets.

    5.1.- Ana _____ trabaja los domingos. (nadie, nunca, siempre)

    5.2.- Ellos _____ hablan francés. (no, ningún, sí)

    5.3.- _____ perro es malo. (jamás, no, ningún)

    5.4.- _____ vino a mi fiesta. (jamás, si, nadie)

    5.5.- Antonio _____ habla mal. (no, nadie, ningún)

    5.6.- En mi casa _____ come sushi. (ningún, algunos, nadie)

    5.7.- Laura y María _____ juegan al fútbol. (nadie, ningún, nunca)

    5.8.- Yo _____ duermo en el piso. (sí, siempre, no)

    5.9.- Mi esposa _____ bebe cerveza. (nadie, ningún, tampoco)

    5.10.- Vosotros _____ escribiréis en mandarín. (jamás, siempre, nadie)

Translations:

Translate the following sentences into English:

1.- El equipo de Liverpool **jamás** caminará solo.

_____

2.- Yo **no** dejaré de amarte.

_____

3.- **Nunca** olvidaré mi país.

_____

4.- **No** podemos dejar de estudiar.

_____

5.- **No** fumo, **tampoco** bebo licor.

_____

6.- En mi calle **nadie** hace fiestas.

_____

7.- Por favor **no** entrar.

_____

8.- **No** tire basura al piso.

_____

9.- Mi hermano **no** está trabajando.

_____

10.- Aprender español **no** es difícil.

_____

Story:

Hay una vieja **leyenda** sobre un **águila** mágica que puede **conceder deseos**. Es una **leyenda** muy, muy vieja. En los últimos doscientos años, nadie ha vuelto a ver a esa **mítica ave**. Sin embargo, no hay nada imposible en el mundo, y una joven llamada Jane se encontró un día al **águila**. Jane estaba caminando por una montaña, y cuando se sentó a descansar, se encontró con el **ave**. "¡Eres tú!" dijo Jane, "Eres el **águila** mágica que puede **conceder deseos**." "No, no lo soy", respondió el ave. "Si, si lo eres. Las **águilas** normales no hablan."

El **águila** tuvo que admitir sus cualidades mágicas, pero aun así se resistió. "Jamás volveré a **conceder deseos**. El mundo se ha vuelto demasiado sencillo. Si deseas algo, seguramente puedes conseguirlo sin mi ayuda. ¿Qué podrías querer? **¿Dinero? ¿Conocimiento? ¿Amigos?** Cualquiera puede inventar algo y volverse millonario, los libros se pueden conseguir gratis, y el internet te conecta con **amigos** del otro lado del planeta. No te tengo que **conceder** ningún **deseo**," dijo el **águila**, sin saber que se equivocaba. "¿Acaso nunca nadie deseó intercambiar de lugar contigo?" preguntó Jane, sorprendiendo al **ave**, que siempre quiso experimentar como eran en verdad las vidas de los seres humanos.

Vocabulary:

1. Leyenda – Legend
2. Águila – Eagle
3. Conceder – Grant
4. Deseos – Wishes
5. Mítica – Mythical
6. Ave – Bird
7. Admitir – Admit
8. Dinero – Money
9. Conocimiento – Knowledge
10. Amigos – Friends

Translated Story:

There is an old **legend** about a magical **eagle** that can **grant wishes**. It is a very, very old **legend**. In the last two hundred years, no one has seen that **mythical bird** again. However, there is nothing impossible in the world, and a young woman named Jane encountered the **eagle** one day. Jane was walking up a mountain, and when she sat down to rest, she encountered the **bird**. "It's you!" Jane said, "You are the magical **eagle** that can **grant wishes**." "No, I am not," replied the **bird**. "Yes, yes you are. Normal **eagles** don't speak."

The **eagle** had to **admit** its magical qualities, but still resisted. "I will never **grant wishes** again. The world has become too simple. If you want something, surely you can get it without my help. What could you want? **Money**? **Knowledge**? **Friends**? Anyone can invent something and become a millionaire, books are available for free, and the internet connects you with **friends** on the other side of the planet. I don't have to **grant** you any **wish**," said the **eagle**, not knowing that it was wrong. "Didn't anyone ever wish to swap places with you?" Jane asked, surprising the **bird**, who always wanted to experience what human lives were really like.

Questions:

1. ¿Qué puede hacer el águila? _____

   What can the eagle do?

2. ¿Hace cuántos años nadie ve al ave? _____

   How many years have passed since someone last saw the bird?

3. ¿Dónde estaba Jane? _____

   Where was Jane?

4. ¿Qué no pueden hacer las águilas normales? _____

   What can't normal eagles do?

5. ¿Qué se puede conseguir gratis? _____

   What can you get for free?

6. ¿Con quién quería cambiar de lugar Jane? _____

   Who does Jane want to change place with?

Answers:

1.1.- no

1.2.- nunca

1.3.- jamás

1.4.- tampoco

1.5.- no

1.6.- Nadie

1.7.- no

1.8.- Ningún

1.9.- no

1.10.- Nadie

2.1.- Yo no trabajo hoy.

2.2.- Ana no baila mal.

2.3.- Ella nunca ha venido aquí.

2.4.- Nosotros nunca jugamos al básquetbol.

2.5.- Nadie vino a la reunión.

2.6.- Ningún alumno estudió.

2.7.- El carro no está limpio.

2.8.- Mi hermano tampoco bebe soda.

2.9.- Tú jamás me olvidarás.

2.10.- No me gusta el sushi.

3.1.- b

3.2.- a

3.3.- b

3.4.- b

3.5.- a

3.6.- b

3.7.- b

3.8.- a

3.9.- b

3.10.- a

4.1.- a

4.2.- a

4.3.- c

4.4.- b

4.5.- a

4.6.- c

4.7.- a

4.8.- c

4.9.- b

4.10.- c

5.1.- nunca

5.2.- no

5.3.- Ningún

5.4.- Nadie

5.5.- no

5.6.- nadie

5.7.- nunca

5.8.- no

5.9.- tampoco

5.10.- jamás

Translations:

1.- The Liverpool team will **never** walk alone.

2.- I will **not** stop loving you.

3.- I will **never** forget my country.

4.- We can**not** stop studying.

5.- I **don't** smoke, I don't drink liquor **either.**

6.- **Nobody** has parties on my street.

7.- Please **do not** enter.

8.- **Do not** throw garbage on the floor.

9.- My brother is **not** working.

10.- Learning Spanish is **not** difficult.

Story:

1. Conceder deseos. – Grant wishes.

2. Doscientos años. – Two hundred years.

3. En la montaña. – On the mountain.

4. Hablar. – Speak.

5. Libros. – Books.

6. Con el águila. – With the eagle.

Chapter 17

SINGULAR AND PLURAL

Welcome to Chapter 17, where we will deal with singular and plural words. In Spanish, nouns, articles and adjectives have gender (masculine and feminine) and, in this case, grammatical number, which is singular and plural.

To write a noun or adjective in plural we must follow some basic rules that we will explain below and, as always, with some simple examples.

First Rule: The letter **S** is added to the plural when the word ends in an atonic vowel (without an accent).

Examples:

Singular	Plural
1. - Él tiene una casa.	- Él tiene 3 casas.
- He has a house.	- He has 3 houses.
2. - Hay una mesa en la sala.	- Hay 2 mesas en la sala.
- There is a table in the room.	- There are 2 tables in the room.
3. - Yo leí un libro.	- Yo leí 2 libros.
- I read a book.	- I read two books.

Second Rule: The letters **ES** are added to the plural when the word ends in a consonant.

Examples:

Singular	Plural
1. - Tengo un papel.	- Tengo 2 papeles.
- I have a paper.	- I have 2 papers.
2. - Ella cantó una canción.	- Ella cantó 3 canciones.
- She sang a song.	- She sang 3 songs.
3. - Pintamos una pared.	- Pintamos 2 paredes.
- We painted a wall.	- We painted 2 walls.

Third Rule: If the word ends in the consonant Z, change the Z to **C** before adding **ES**.

Examples:

Singular	Plural
1. - ¡Qué bonita luz!	- ¡Qué bonitas lu**ces**!
- What a beautiful light!	- What beautiful light**s**!
2. - Él dibujó una cruz.	- Él dibujó 5 cru**ces**.
- He drew a cross.	- He drew 5 cross**es**.
3. - Yo compré un lápiz.	- Yo compré 4 lápi**ces**.
- I bought a pencil.	- I bought 4 pencil**s**.

Fourth Rule: Words that end in **S** or **X** are written the same in singular and plural.

Examples:

Singular	Plural
1. - Examinó el **tórax** del paciente.	- Examinó los **tórax** de los pacientes.
- He examined the **chest** of the patient.	- He examined the **chests** of the patients.
2. - Yo sembré un **cactus**.	- Yo sembré 6 **cactus**.
- I planted a **cactus**.	- I planted 6 **cacti**.
3. - Nosotros tuvimos una **crisis**.	- Nosotros tuvimos muchas **crisis**.
- We had a **crisis**.	- We had a lot of **crises**.

Exercises:

1.- Convert the following words to their plural form.

        1.1.- Voz   _____

        1.2.- Beso   _____

        1.3.- Amor   _____

        1.4.- Dolor   _____

        1.5.- Mesa   _____

        1.6.- Rey   _____

        1.7.- Clímax   _____

        1.8.- Corazón   _____

        1.9.- Maestro   _____

        1.10.- Alumno   _____

2.- Convert the following words to their singular form.

        2.1.- Virus   _____

        2.2.- Lápices   _____

        2.3.- Computadoras   _____

        2.4.- Árboles   _____

        2.5.- Dedos   _____

        2.6.- Quesos   _____

        2.7.- Luces   _____

        2.8.- Pelotas   _____

        2.9.- Libros   _____

        2.10.- Pantalones   _____

3.- Select the correct word in plural.

        3.1.- Perdiz

        a.- Perdices

        b.- Perdises

        3.2.- Color

        a.- Colors

        b.- Colores

        3.3.- Taxi

        a.- Taxises

        b.- Taxis

        3.4.- Puerta

        a.- Puertas

        b.- Puertases

        3.5.- Cuaderno

        a.- Cuadernos

        b.- Cuadernoses

        3.6.- Español

        a.- Españoleses

        b.- Españoles

        3.7.- Zapato

        a.- Zapatoz

        b.- Zapatos

3.8.- Moneda

a.- Monedas

b.- Monedax

3.9.- Ley

a.- Leyeses

b.- Leyes

3.10.- León

a.- Leones

b.- Leoneses

4.- Select the correct word in singular form.

4.1.- Cicatrices

a.- Cicatriz

b.- Cicatrice

4.2.- Ustedes

a.- Usted

b.- Ustes

4.3.- Ratones

a.- Rato

b.- Ratón

4.4.- Noches

a.- Nocheses

b.- Noche

4.5.- Lombrices

a.- Lombriz

b.- Lombrice

4.6.- Números

a.- Número

b.- Númers

4.7.- Virus

a.- Viru

b.- Virus

4.8.- Capitanes

a.- Capitán

b.- Capitano

4.9.- Papeles

a.- Papele

b.- Papel

4.10.- Cines

a.- Cine

b.- Cin

5.- Complete the sentences to change them to singular or plural, depending on the case.

5.1- Tengo una camisa. / Tengo 4 _____.

5.2. Ella comió una _____. / Ella comió 2 tortas.

5.3.- Una bonita casa. / Dos bonitas _____.

5.4.- Escuché una voz. / Escuché varias _____.

5.5.- Vimos una _____. / Vimos muchas luces.

5.6.- Tomaron una taza de café. / Tomaron dos _____ de café.

5.7.- Tuvo una _____. / Tuvo dos crisis.

5.8.- Entre _____. / Entre paréntesis.

5.9.- Es mi amor. / Son mis _____.

5.10.- Tocaron la puerta. / Tocaron las _____.

Translations:

Translate the following sentences into English:

1.- Un sombrero, dos camisas, tres pantalones.

_____

2.- Eran rojos, redondos, duros y pesados.

_____

3.- Ana tenía los ojos negros como dos carbones.

_____

4.- Las casas estaban abandonadas.

_____

5.- Mis hermanos son mis amigos.

_____

6.- Peleaban como perros y gatos.

_____

7.- Las funciones son a las 7pm todos los días.

_____

8.- Hablar varios idiomas y conocer nuevas culturas.

_____

9.- Las mejores vacaciones de mi vida.

_____

10.- Leer buenos libros y escuchar buena música.

_____

Story:

Había una vez un científico llamado Joseph, pero todos lo conocían como Joe el **Cavernícola**. La verdad no era un **sobrenombre** muy **halagador** para un científico. Ese nombre se debía a que Joe había escogido un proyecto muy particular. Joe decidió que iba a dedicar su vida de **investigación** y de ciencia a recrear todos los grandes **logros** de la humanidad, tal como habían sucedido. Esto significa que pasó varios años descubriendo como por primera vez el fuego, la **rueda**, y los metales. Por eso es que los otros científicos lo llamaban **cavernícola**.

A pesar de las burlas, la verdad es que Joe alcanzó grandes **logros**. Sí, tal vez nadie necesitaba que alguien volviera a **inventar** el papel o aprendiera a domesticar **caballos**. Pero, son cosas que tomamos por seguro en el siglo veintiuno, sin **comprender** lo difíciles que fueron en su momento. El hecho de que Joe el **Cavernícola** podía tomar fotos y grabar todo lo que podía descubrir e **inventar** como si fuera la primera vez, bueno, eso sí era una muy interesante novedad. Así fue como conseguimos un video de cómo se pudo **inventar** las fotos, y pudimos ver en vivo como Joe creó un **bombillo** por primera vez.

Vocabulary:

1. Cavernícola – Caveman
2. Sobrenombre – Nickname
3. Halagador – Flattering
4. Investigación – Research
5. Logros – Achievements
6. Rueda - Wheel
7. Inventar - Invent
8. Caballos - Horses
9. Comprender - Understanding
10. Bombillo - Light bulb

Translated Story:

Once upon a time there was a scientist named Joseph, but everyone knew him as **Caveman** Joe. The truth is that was not a very **flattering nickname** for a scientist. That name was because Joe had chosen a very particular project. Joe decided that he was going to dedicate his life of **research** and science to recreating all the great **achievements** of humanity, as they had happened. This means that he spent several years discovering fire, the **wheel**, and metals for the first time. That's why the other scientists called him a **caveman**.

Despite the teasing, the truth is that Joe accomplished great **achievements**. Yes, maybe no one needed someone to **invent** paper or learn to tame **horses** again. But they are things we take for granted in the twenty-first century, without **understanding** how difficult they were at the time. The fact that **Caveman** Joe could take pictures and record everything he could discover and **invent** as if it were the first time, well, that was a very interesting novelty. This is how we got a video of how it had been possible to **invent** photos, and we were able to see live how Joe created a **light bulb** for the first time.

Questions:

1. ¿Cuál era el sobrenombre de Joseph? _____

   What was Joseph's nickname?

2. ¿Qué era Joseph? _____

   What was Joseph?

3. ¿Qué tardó varios años en descubrir? _____

   What did he take several years to discover?

4. ¿Qué alcanzó Joe? _____

   What did Joe accomplish?

5. ¿Qué aprendió a domesticar? _____

   What did he learn to tame?

6. ¿De qué había un video? _____

   What was there a video of?

Answers:

1.1.- Voces

1.2.- Besos

1.3.- Amores

1.4.- Dolores

1.5.- Mesas

1.6.- Reyes

1.7.- Clímax

1.8.- Corazones

1.9.- Maestros

1.10.- Alumnos

2.1.- Virus

2.2.- Lápiz

2.3.- Computadora

2.4.-Árbol

2.5.- Dedo

2.6.- Queso

2.7.- Luz

2.8.- Pelota

2.9.- Libro

2.10.- Pantalón

3.1.- a

3.2- b

3.3.- b

3.4.- a

3.5.- a

3.6.- b

3.7.- b

3.8.- a

3.9.- b

3.10.- a

4.1.- a

4.2.- a

4.3.- b

4.4.- b

4.5.- a

4.6.- a

4.7.- b

4.8.- a

4.9.- b

4.10.- a

5.1.- camisas

5.2.- torta

5.3.- casas

5.4.- voces

5.5.- luz

5.6.- tazas

5.7.- crisis

5.8.- paréntesis

5.9.- amores

5.10.- puertas

Translations:

1. A hat, two shirts, and three pants.

2.- They were red, round, hard and heavy.

3. Ana had black eyes like two coals.

4. The houses were abandoned.

5. My brothers are my friends.

6. They fought like cats and dogs.

7. The functions are at 7pm every day.

8. Speak various languages and meet new cultures.

9. The best holidays of my life.

10. Read good books and listen to good music.

Story:

1. Joe el Cavernícola. – Joe the Caveman.

2. Un científico. – A scientist.

3. El fuego, la rueda y los metales. – Fire, the wheel and metals.

4. Grandes logros. – Big acheivements.

5. Caballos. – Horses.

6. De cómo se pudo inventar las fotos. – Of how they could invent photos.

Chapter 18
PROFESSIONS

In Chapter 1, we learned how to greet people in Spanish, but it is common on first meeting someone to ask questions such as, 'What is your profession?', 'What do you do?' or 'What field do you work in?'. In this chapter, we are going to learn how to talk about the most common professions and jobs in Spanish.

Here is a list of some of those professions and jobs:
- Abogado - Lawyer
- Arquitecto - Architect
- Atleta - Athlete
- Bombero - Fireman
- Botones - Bellboy
- Camarero - Waiter
- Chofer - Driver
- Cirujano - Surgeon
- Cocinero - Cook
- Deportista - Athlete
- Enfermero - Nurse
- Escritor - Writer
- Ingeniero - Engineer
- Médico - Doctor
- Policía - Policeman
- Profesor - Professor
- Taxista - Taxi driver

There are a number of norms regarding gender in some professions that we are going to review with examples.

For nouns whose masculine form ends in the vowel "**o**", the feminine is formed by substituting it for the vowel "**a**" (except "model - modelo" which is written the same for both genders).

Examples:

Male	Female
Firefighter:	
- Bombero	- Bomber**a**
Engineer:	
- Ingeniero	- Ingenier**a**
Teacher:	
- Maestro	- Maestr**a**

Nouns ending in the vowel "**a**" in the masculine form are usually spelled the same for both genders.

Examples:

Male	Female
Athlete:	
- Atleta	- Atleta
Pediatrician:	
- Pediatra	- Pediatra
Masseuse:	
- Masajista	- Masajista

Those that end in "**or**" in the masculine form are changed to feminine by adding the vowel "**a**" at the end.

Examples:

Male	Female
Professor:	
- Profesor	- Profesor**a**
Designer:	
- Diseñador	- Diseñador**a**
Writer:	
- Escritor	- Escritor**a**

_____

Exercises:

1.- Select the profession or trade according to the description.

1.1.- This person heals ill people.

a.- Abogado

b.- Profesor

c.- Médico

1.2.- This person fights fire.

a.- Atleta

b.- Bombero

c.- Botones

1.3.- This person drives the bus.

a.- Cocinero

b.- Escritor

c.- Chofer

1.4.- This person draws blueprints.

a.- Arquitecto

b.- Policía

c.- Taxista

1.5.- This person prepares dinner.

a.- Abogado

b.- Cocinera

c.- Masajista

1.6.- This person fights crime.

a.- Botones

b.- Chofer

c.- Policía

1.7.- She defends you in court.

a.- Abogada

b.- Camarero

c.- Pediatra

1.8.- He helps us with our bags at the hotel.

a.- Bombero

b.- Cirujano

c.- Botones

1.9.- This person competes in the Olympics.

a.- Abogado

b.- Chofer

c.- Atleta

1.10.- He brings us our food in the restaurant.

a.- Camarero

b.- Taxista

c.- Arquitecto

2.- Write the following professions and jobs in the female form.

2.1.- Medico   _____

2.2.- Cocinero   _____

2.3.- Taxista   _____

2.4.- Abogado   _____

2.5.- Profesor   _____

2.6.- Pediatra   _____

2.7.- Camarero   _____

2.8.- Ingeniero   _____

2.9.- Bombero   _____

2.10.- Atleta   _____

3.- Write the name of the profession or trade in Spanish.

3.1.- Athlete   _____

3.2.- Writer   _____

3.3.- Surgeon   _____

3.4.- Female Nurse   _____

3.5.- Engineer   _____

3.6.- Bellboy   _____

3.7.- Teacher   _____

3.8.- Lawyer   _____

3.9.- Female Doctor   _____

3.10.- Taxi driver   _____

4.- According to the description, select the profession or trade from the right column.

4.1.- Takes care of the sick.	A.- Ingeniero
4.2.- Teaches classes.	B.- Atleta
4.3.- Writes novels.	C.- Cocinero
4.4.- Plays in a stadium.	D.- Botones
4.5.- Operates in an operating room.	E.- Abogado
4.6.- Constructs buildings.	F.- Taxista

4.7.- Works in the kitchen.	G.- Escritor
4.8.- Drives a taxi.	H.- Enfermero
4.9.- Knows the law.	I.- Cirujano
4.10.- Carries suitcases.	J.- Profesor

5.- Answer true (V = **Verdad**) or false (F = **Falso**) for the following statements:

5.1.- Bombero: Puts out fires.

    F

    V

5.2.- Cirujano: Drives a taxi.

    F

    V

5.3.- Maestro: Cooks lunch.

    F

    V

5.4.- Abogado: Takes care of the sick.

    F

    V

5.5.- Arquitecto: Designs houses.

    F

    V

5.6.- Camarero: Waits tables.

    F

    V

5.7.- Policía: Drives a bus.

    F

    V

5.8.- Bell boy: Carries suitcases.

    F

V

5.9.- Taxista: Operates in an operating room.

F

V

5.10.- Atleta: Participates in the Olympics.

F

V

Translations:

Translate the following sentences into English:

1.- Los **bomberos** son héroes sin capas.

_____

2.- El **policía** detuvo un peligroso ladrón.

_____

3.- Nuestro **cocinero** es el mejor del mundo.

_____

4.- Mi esposa es una excelente **médica**.

_____

5.- Mi hija será una gran **escritora**.

_____

6.- Yo fui **profesor** durante 25 años.

_____

7.- Antonio es un buen **ingeniero**.

_____

8.- Los **taxistas** de mi ciudad hablan de todo.

_____

9.- Juan fue el mejor **arquitecto**.

_____

10.- Los **enfermeros** tienen un gran corazón.

_____

Story:

Ser **piloto** de avión no es un trabajo sencillo. Para convertirse en **piloto** hay que estudiar mucho, ser **valiente**, **inteligente**, y talentoso. Todo eso lo ponen aprueba en muchos **exámenes** que los candidatos tienen que pasar para alcanzar sus **sueños**. Pero, hay un rumor de que uno de los exámenes es muy interesante, algo divertido, un poco **raro**, simplemente inesperado.

Algunos **pilotos** cuentan la historia de que uno de sus **exámenes** era como **sobrevivir** en una isla desierta en caso de que el avión se estrellara. Sin embargo, el **examen** tenía dos partes. La primera era muy seria, y ponía a prueba todos sus conocimientos. Pero, la segunda parte, era casi un juego que ponía a prueba la imaginación de los **pilotos**.

Una de las preguntas era, que tipo de persona preferirían llevar con ustedes en caso de terminar en una isla desierta. Las opciones lógicas eran un doctor, tal vez un atleta en buenas condiciones físicas, o incluso un fuerte **obrero** que pueda construir un refugio. Sin embargo, había opciones diferentes, como un biólogo que identifique frutas venenosas, un **carnicero** que pueda cazar animales, o un comediante para **mantener** a todos entretenidos.

Vocabulary:

1. Piloto – Pilot
2. Valiente – Brave
3. Inteligente – Smart
4. Exámenes – Exams
5. Sueños – Dreams
6. Raro – Weird
7. Sobrevivir – Survive
8. Obrero – Construction worker
9. Carnicero – Butcher
10. Mantener – Keep

Translated Story:

Being an airplane **pilot** is not an easy job. To become a **pilot,** you have to study hard, be **brave**, **smart**, and talented. All of that is tested in many **exams** that candidates have to pass to achieve their **dreams**. But there is a rumor that one of the **exams** is very interesting, somewhat funny, a little **weird**; simply unexpected.

Some **pilots** tell the story that one of their **exams** was how to **survive** on a desert island in case the plane crashed. However, the exam had two parts. The first was very serious, and it tested all their knowledge. But the second part was almost a game that put the **pilots'** imagination to the test.

One of the questions was, what kind of person would you prefer to take with you if you ended up on a desert island. The logical choices were a doctor, perhaps an athlete in good physical condition, or even a strong **construction worker** who can build a shelter. However, there were different options, such as a biologist who identifies poisonous fruits, a **butcher** who can hunt animals, or a comedian to **keep** everyone entertained.

Questions:

1. ¿Quiénes tienen que ser valientes, inteligentes y talentosos? _____
   Who has to be brave, intelligent and talented?

2. ¿Cuántos exámenes tienen que pasar? _____
   How many exams do they have to pass?

3. ¿Dónde tienen que sobrevivir? _____
   Where do they have to survive?

4. ¿Cuántas partes tenía el exámen? _____
   How many parts did the exam have?

5. ¿Quién es fuerte? _____
   Who is strong?

6. ¿Quién puede cazar?_____
   Who can hunt?

Answers:

1.1.- c

1.2.- b

1.3.- c

1.4.- a

1.5.- b

1.6.- c

1.7.- a

1.8.- c

1.9.- c

1.10.- a

2.1.- Médica

2.2.- Cocinera

2.3.- Taxista

2.4.- Abogada

2.5.- Profesora

2.6.- Pediatra

2.7.- Camarera

2.8.- Ingeniera

2.9.- Bombera

2.10.- Atleta

3.1.- Atleta

3.2.- Escritor

3.3.- Cirujano

3.4.- Enfermera

3.5.- Ingeniero

3.6.- Botones

3.7.- Maestro

3.8.- Abogado

3.9.- Médica

3.10.- Taxista

4.1.- H

4.2.- J

4.3.- G

4.4.- B

4.5.- I

4.6.- A

4.7.- C

4.8.- F

4.9.- E

4.10.- D

5.1.- V

5.2.- F

5.3.- F

5.4.- F

5.5.- V

5.6.- V

5.7.- F

5.8.- V

5.9.- F

5.10.- V

Translations:

1.- **Firefighters** are heroes without capes.

2.- The **policeman** stopped a dangerous thief.

3.- Our **cook** is the best in the world.

4.- My wife is an excellent **doctor**.

5.- My daughter will be a great **writer**.

6.- I was a **teacher** for 25 years.

7.- Antonio is a good **engineer**.

8.- The **taxi drivers** in my city talk about everything.

9.- Juan was the best **architect**.

10.- **Nurses** have a big heart.

Story:

1. Los pilotos de avión. – Airplane pilots.

2. Muchos. – Many.

3. En una isla desierta. – On a desert island.

4. Dos. – Two.

5. Un obrero. – A construction worker.

6. Un carnicero. – A butcher.

Chapter 19

THE FAMILY

The first people to support you and to rejoice because you speak Spanish are undoubtedly members of your family, so the least we can do is learn how to identify the correct terms for the family in Spanish. That is why we are going to review the denomination of the family in this chapter.

Here is a list of the Spanish forms of the closest familial relatives:

- Madre / Mamá - Mother / Mom
- Padre / Papá - Father / Dad
- Hermano - Brother
- Hermana - Sister
- Hermanos - Siblings
- Hijo - Son
- Hija - Daughter
- Abuelo - Grandfather
- Abuela - Grandmother
- Nieto - Grandson
- Nieta - Granddaughter
- Tío - Uncle
- Tía - Aunt
- Primo / Prima - Cousin
- Esposo - Husband
- Esposa - Wife
- Cuñado - Brother-in-law
- Cuñada - Sister-in-law
- Yerno - Son-in-law

- Nuera - Daughter-in-law

- Suegro - Father-in-law

- Suegra - Mother-in-law

- Bisabuelo - Great-grandfather

- Bisabuela - Great-grandmother

- Bisnieto - Great-grandson

- Bisnieta - Great-granddaughter

- Padrastro - Stepfather

- Madrastra - Stepmother

- Hijastro - Stepson

- Hijastra - Stepdaughter

- Hermanastro - Stepbrother

- Hermanastra - Stepsister

Examples:

1. - El **hermano** de Pedro es bombero.

   - Pedro's **brother** is a firefighter.

2. - Mi **abuela** cumpleaños el 2 de mayo.

   - My **grandmother's** birthday is on May 2.

3. - El **suegro** de María es alto.

   - Maria's **father-in-law** is tall.

The marital statuses in Spanish are:

- Casado / Casada - Married

- Soltero / Soltera - Single

- Divorciado / Divorciado - Divorced

- Viudo / Viuda - Widowed

<u>Examples</u>:

1. - Estoy **casado** desde hace 25 años.

   - I have been **married** for 25 years.

2. - Gabriela es **soltera**.

   - Gabriela is **single**.

3. - Mis padres están **divorciados**.

   - My parents are **divorced**.

———————————

Exercises:

1.- Write the family member or marital status in Spanish.

    1.1.- Mother   _____

    1.2.- Wife   _____

    1.3.- Daughter   _____

    1.4.- Brother-in-law   _____

    1.5.- Grandfather   _____

    1.6.- Single   _____

    1.7.- Brother-in-law   _____

    1.8.- Widow   _____

    1.9.- Brother   _____

    1.10.- Uncle   _____

2.- Answer the following questions in Spanish.

    2.1.- My wife's brother is my _____.

    2.2.- My aunt's daughter is my _____.

    2.3.- My husband's father is my _____.

    2.4.- My father's sister is my _____.

    2.5.- My mother's father is my _____.

    2.6.- Your brother's wife is your _____.

    2.7.- Your daughter's son is your _____.

    2.8.- My parent's other children are my _____.

    2.9.- My son's wife is my _____.

    2.10.- My father's grandfather is my _____.

3.- Select the correct family member from the right column.

    3.1.- Mother's brother   A.- Cuñada

    3.2.- Son of uncle   B.- Tía

3.3.- Father's mother	C.- Nieta
3.4.- Brother's wife	D.- Bisabuela
3.5.- Mother of the husband	E.- Madrastra
3.6.- Grandmother of mother	F.- Abuelo
3.7.- Wife of father	G.- Abuela
3.8.- Father of father	H.- Tío
3.9.- Daughter of daughter	I.- Suegra
3.10.- Sister of Father	J.- Primo

4.- Write in English the corresponding family member or marital status

4.1.- Cuñada   _____

4.2.- Soltero   _____

4.3.- Abuelo   _____

4.4.- Madre   _____

4.5.- Tío   _____

4.6.- Papá   _____

4.7.- Hermano   _____

4.8.- Padrastro   _____

4.9.- Yerno   _____

4.10.- Esposa   _____

5.- Select the correct option.

    5.1.- Madre is

        a.- Father

        b.- Grandmother

        c.- Mother

5.2.- Bisabuelo is

        a.- Great-grandfather

        b.- Grandfather

        c.- Great-grandmother

5.3.- Cuñada is

        a.- Sister

        b.- Prima

        c.- sister-in-law

5.4.- Esposo is

        a.- Grandfather

        b.- Uncle

        c.- Husband

5.5.- Divorciado is

        a.- Married

        b.- Widow

        c.- Divorced

5.6.- Primo is

        a.- Uncle

        b.- Cousin

        c.- Brother

5.7.- Viudo is

        a.- Widower

        b.- Married

        c.- Single

5.8.- Madrastra is

      a.- Mother

      b.- Stepmother

      c.- Mom

5.9.- Soltero is

      a.- Married

      b.- Single

      c.- Widow

5.10.- Papá is

      a.- Mom

      b.- Father

      c.- Dad

Translations:

Translate the following sentences into English:

1.- Mi **mamá** fue una gran mujer.

_____

2.- Tu **padre** Juan es un buen arquitecto.

_____

3.- A mi **esposa** le gusta el café muy caliente.

_____

4.- Ellos se **divorciaron** hace un año.

_____

5.- Mi **hija** habla inglés y español.

_____

6.- Es mejor la vida de **casado** que la de **soltero**.

_____

7.- Los **hermanos** deben ser unidos.

_____

8.- Yo sí tuve una buena **suegra**.

_____

9.- Los **primos** son los primeros amigos.

_____

10.- Mi **abuelo** trabajó en el campo toda su vida.

_____

Story:

Esta es una historia de misterio. Pero, también es un cuento divertido. Eso es lo que pasa cuando se pierde un objeto **valioso** durante una **fiesta** familiar. Sin embargo, este evento no requería **pelear** y buscar un detective **privado**. Resulta que mi familia es muy grande, pero todos nos queremos mucho. Todos los miembros de la familia son muy unidos. Nadie de verdad pensaba que algún primo o cuñado pudiera robarlos. Así que cuando la tía favorita de todos, Anita, **exclamó** en **medio** de la sala "¡Perdí mi posesión más **valiosa**!" En lugar de **pelear** y gritar, toda la familia se organizó para trabajar juntos para encontrar el objeto perdido.

Uno de mis primos se acercó a Anita, quien era su mamá, y le dijo, "Yo soy lo más **valioso** para ti, y **aquí** estoy." Pero Anita seguía buscando. Su hermana encontró el abrigo de mi abuela, la mamá de mis tías. Pero eso tampoco era lo que Anita buscaba. Su nuera intentó preguntarle que buscaba, pero Anita no quiso responderle. Hasta que finalmente todos juntos preguntamos, "¿Qué se te perdió?" Eso hizo a mi tía **reaccionar**. "¡Mi **vaso** de vino!" **exclamó**. Y, **obviamente**, todo este tiempo tenía el **vaso** de vino en la mano. Tal vez fue demasiado vino.

Vocabulary:

1. Valioso – Valuable
2. Fiesta – Party
3. Pelear – Fighting
4. Privado – Private
5. Medio – Middle
6. Exclamó – Exclaimed
7. Aquí – Here
8. Reaccionar – React
9. Vaso – Glass
10. Obviamente – Obviously

Translated Story:

This is a mystery story. But it is also a funny story. That's what happens when a **valuable** item is lost during a family **party**. However, this event did not require **fighting** or searching for a **private** detective. It turns out that my family is very large, but we all love each other very much. All members of the family are very close. No one really thought that a cousin or brother-in-law could steal from them. So, when everyone's favorite aunt Anita **exclaimed** in the **middle** of the room "I lost my most **valuable** possession!" Instead of **fighting** and yelling, the whole family organized to work together to find the lost item.

One of my cousins approached Anita, who was her mother, and said, "I am the most precious thing for you and **here** I am." But Anita kept looking. Her sister found my grandmother's coat, my aunts' mother. But that wasn't what Anita was looking for either. Her daughter-in-law tried to ask her what she was looking for, but Anita didn't want to answer her. Until finally all together we asked, "What did you lose?" That made my aunt **react**. "My **glass** of wine!" she **exclaimed**. And, **obviously**, all this time she had the wine **glass** in her hand. Maybe it was too much wine.

Questions:

1. ¿Qué se perdió? _____

   What was lost?

2. ¿Durante qué evento se perdió? _____

   During what event was it lost?

3. ¿A quién se le perdió? _____

   Who lost it?

4. ¿De quién era el abrigo? _____

   Whose was the coat?

5. ¿A quién no le respondió Anita? _____

   Who did Anita not respond to?

6. ¿Quién tenía el objeto perdido? _____

   Who had the lost object?

Answers:

1.1.- Madre

1.2.- Esposa

1.3.- Hija

1.4.- Cuñado

1.5.- Abuelo

1.6.- Soltero / Soltera

1.7.- Cuñado

1.8.- Viuda / Viudo

1.9.- Hermano

1.10.- Tío

2.1.- cuñado

2.2.- prima

2.3.- suegro

2.4.- tía

2.5.- abuelo

2.6.- cuñada

2.7.- nieto

2.8.- hermanos

2.9.- nuera

2.10.- bisabuelo

3.1.- H

3.2.- J

3.3.- G

3.4.- A

3.5.- I

3.6.- D

3.7.- E

3.8.- F

3.9.- C

3.10.- B

4.1.- Sister-in-law

4.2.- Single

4.3.- Grandfather

4.4.- Mother

4.5.- Uncle

4.6.- Dad

4.7.- Brother

4.8.- Stepfather

4.9.- Son-in-law

4.10.- Wife

5.1.- c

5.2.- a

5.3.- c

5.4.- c

5.5.- c

5.6.- b

5.7.- a

5.8.- b

5.9.- b

5.10.- c

Translations:

1.- My **mother** was a great woman.

2.- Your **father** Juan is a good architect.

3.- My **wife** likes very hot coffee.

4.- They got **divorced** a year ago.

5.- My **daughter** speaks English and Spanish.

6.- **Married** life is better than **single life**.

7.- **Brothers/Siblings** must be united.

8.- I did have a good **mother-in-law**.

9.- **Cousins** are the first friends.

10.- My **grandfather** worked in the countryside all his life.

Story:

1. Un objeto valioso. – A valuable object.

2. Una fiesta familiar. – A family party.

3. A Anita. – Anita.

4. De la abuela. – The grandmother's.

5. A su nuera. – Her daugher-in-law.

6. Anita. – Anita.

Chapter 20

THE HUMAN BODY

When traveling to a Spanish-speaking country and making friends, they will probably ask you what your relatives and acquaintances in your country look like, so you will have to describe them. To do that, you need to know the basic vocabulary of the parts of the human body. In this chapter, we are going to learn this and, as always, use examples and exercises so that you can describe the human body in Spanish.

Here is a list of some parts of the body:
- Cabeza - Head
- Cabello - Hair
- Orejas - Ears
- Ojos - Eyes
- Cejas - Eyebrows
- Pestañas - Eyelashes
- Nariz - Nose
- Boca - Mouth
- Labios - Lips
- Dientes - Teeth
- Lengua - Tongue
- Cuello - Neck
- Espalda - Back
- Tórax - Chest
- Abdomen - Abdomen
- Hombro - Shoulder
- Brazo - Arm
- Codo - Elbow
- Muñeca - Wrist

- Mano - Hand
- Dedos de la Mano - Fingers
- Uñas - Nails
- Cadera - Waist
- Pierna - Leg
- Rodilla - Knee
- Tobillo - Ankle
- Pie - Foot
- Dedos del Pie - Toes

Examples:

1. - Ella tenía los **ojos** negros.

   - She had black **eyes**.

2. - Ella tomó el cachorro en sus **manos**.

   - She took the puppy in her **hands**.

3. - Se dobló su **tobillo** al correr.

   - He bent his **ankle** while running.

We will also review some internal organs:

- Cerebro - Brain
- Corazón - Heart
- Pulmones - Lungs
- Estómago - Stomach
- Hígado - Liver
- Riñones - Kidney
- Vejiga - Bladder

Examples:

1. - El sufría de dolores de **estómago**.

   - He suffered from **stomach** aches.

2. - Su **corazón** palpitó con fuerza.

   - His **heart** beat with force.

3. - Sus **pulmones** se llenaron de humo.

   - His **lungs** were filled with smoke.

———————

Exercises:

1.- Complete the following sentences with the body part in Spanish.

    1.1.- She painted her _____ red.

        a.- rodillas

        b.- pulmones

        c.- labios

    1.2.- He closed his _____ tightly so as not to see it.

        a.- orejas

        b.- ojos

        c.- dedos de la mano

    1.3.- He combed his _____ lovingly.

        a.- cabello

        b.- corazón

        c.- cuello

    1.4.- He kneeled on his _____ and bowed before her.

        a.- dientes

        b.- rodillas

        c.- dedos de los pies

    1.5.- She makes my _____ beat.

        a.- corazón

        b.- oreja

        c.- nariz

1.6.- Laura removed the earrings from her _____.

      a.- uñas

      b.- riñón

      c.- orejas

1.7.- He carried the heavy weight on his _____.

      a.- nariz

      b.- vejiga

      c.- espalda

1.8.- She covered her ____ with black gloves.

      a.- orejas

      b.- pulmones

      c.- manos

1.9.- She wore a pearl necklace on her _____.

      a.- cuello

      b.- cadera

      c.- pulmon

1.10.- In which _____ is the wedding ring used?

      a.- riñón

      b.- dedo de la mano

      c.- ojo

2.- Write the following parts of the body in Spanish.

      2.1.- Toes   _____

      2.2.- Liver   _____

      2.3.- Nose   _____

2.4.- Knees   _____

2.5.- Shoulder   _____

2.6.- Teeth   _____

2.7.- Arm   _____

2.8.- Eyelashes   _____

2.9.- Waist   _____

2.10.- Back   _____

3.- Select the organ or body part from the right column that matches the description

3.1.- Organs of respiration	A.- Pies
3.2.- Where earrings go	B.- Dedo de la mano
3.3.- Shoes are worn on your	C.- Ojos
3.4.- Intelligence and memory center	D.- Cabello
3.5.- A ring goes on a	E.- Nariz
3.6.- Pump the blood	F. - Dientes
3.7.- We see with our	G.- Corazón
3.8.- Apparatus of smell	I.- Pulmones
3.9.- We bite with our	J.- Cerebro
3.10.- We comb our	K.- Orejas

4.- Identify each organ or part of the body

4.1.- Cuello   _____

4.2.- Vejiga   _____

4.3.- Tórax   _____

4.4.- Lengua   _____

4.5.- Pulmones   _____

4.6.- Cadera   _____

4.7.- Dedos del Pie   _____

4.8.- Muñeca   _____

4.9.- Uña   _____

4.10.- Labios   _____

5.- Complete the sentence with the options found in parentheses.

    5.1.- The socks go on the _____. (manos, pies, orejas)

    5.2.- The _____ are for kissing. (labios, ojos, tobillos)

    5.3.- The watch goes on the left _____. (rodilla, riñon, muñeca)

    5.4.- Sound enters through the _____.   (pestañas,   orejas, manos)

    5.5.- The tie goes around the _____. (nariz, corazón, cuello)

    5.6.- The gloves are worn on the _____. (cejas, orejas, manos)

    5.7.- We see with our _____. (pulmones, tobillos, ojos)

    5.8.- You have to brush your _____ after eating. (ojos, dientes, pies)

    5.9.- We kneel when bending the _____. (orejas, pestañas, rodillas)

    5.10.- The _____is washed with shampoo. (dedos, higado, cabello)

Translations:

Translate the following sentences into English:

1.- Mi esposa tiene un **cuello** hermoso y delicado.

_____

2.- A ella se le ponen los **ojos** verdes si se enfada.

_____

3.- El **cerebro** tiene que ejercitarse con la lectura.

_____

4.- El hombre debe tener las **uñas** cortas y limpias.

_____

5.- El **tórax** protege al **corazón** y a los **pulmones**.

_____

6.- Tomar suficiente agua ayuda a mantener sanos los **riñones**.

_____

7.- No apoyar los **codos** en la mesa, ni hablar con la **boca** llena.

_____

8.- Sus **pies** parecían no tocar el piso.

_____

9.- Ella acarició su **cabello** con los **dedos de la mano**.

_____

10.- Se frotó las **manos** esperando su regalo.

_____

Story:

A veces, una **historia** nos puede **marcar** de por vida. Una **historia** nos puede **inspirar** y puede cambiarnos como personas. **A veces**, una buena **historia** puede hacernos crear nuevas **historias** increíbles. Pero, a veces, eso puede no ser algo bueno. Todos conocemos la **historia** del **monstruo** de Frankenstein, grande, verde, **aterrador** y construido con varias partes. Esa **historia** influenció mucho a un joven científico que por casualidad se llamaba Frankie. Así que Frankie decidió que él también quería crear un **monstruo**.

Pero, los tiempos cambian. Ya no queremos **monstruos** en nuestros castillos, queremos robots en nuestros apartamentos. Así que Frankie construyó un robot usando partes de muchas cosas diferentes. La cabeza del robot era un televisor, y su corazón era un **reloj**. Los pulmones eran un par de cafeteras, y los pies eran **aspiradoras**. Su espalda tenía muchas **luces** y botones, y su estómago era una gran base de datos. Todas las personas se preguntan si el robot de Frankie funcionó. Nadie ha podido preguntarle, porque Frankie incluyó su único **teléfono** en el robot.

Vocabulary:

1. A veces – Sometimes
2. Historia – Story
3. Marcar – Mark
4. Inspirar – Inspire
5. Monstruo – Monstruo
6. Aterrador – Scary
7. Aspiradora - Vacuum cleaner
8. Reloj – Clock
9. Luces – Lights
10. Teléfono – Phone

Translated Story:

Sometimes a **story** can **mark** us for life. A **story** can **inspire** us and can change us as people. **Sometimes** a good **story** can make us create amazing new **stories**. But **sometimes** that may not be a good thing. We all know the **story** of Frankenstein's **monster**, big, green, **scary**, and built with several parts. That **story** greatly influenced a young scientist who, by coincidence, was named Frankie. So, Frankie decided that he too wanted to create a **monster**.

But times change. We no longer want **monsters** in our castles, we want robots in our apartments. So Frankie built a robot using parts of many different things. The robot's head was a television, and his heart was a **clock**. The lungs were a pair of coffee makers, and the feet were **vacuum cleaners**. His back had many **lights** and buttons, and his stomach was a large database. All the people wonder if Frankie's robot worked. No one has been able to ask him, because Frankie included his only **phone** in the robot.

Questions:

1. ¿Cómo nos marca una historia? _____

   How can a story sometimes mark us?

2. ¿Qué nos puede inspirar a crear? _____

   What can it inspire us to create?

3. ¿Cómo era el monstruo de Frankenstein? _____

   What did Frankenstein's monster look like?

4. ¿Dónde queremos robots? _____

   Where do we want robots?

5. ¿Qué era la cabeza del robot? _____

   What was the head of the robot?

6. ¿Dónde está el teléfono de Frankie? _____

   Where is Frankie's telephone?

Answers:

1.1.- c

1.2.- b

1.3.- a

1.4.- b

1.5.- a

1.6.- c

1.7.- c

1.8.- c

1.9.- a

1.10.- b

2.1.- Dedos del Pie

2.2.- Hígado

2.3.- Nariz

2.4.- Rodillas

2.5.- Hombro

2.6.- Dientes

2.7.- Brazo

2.8.- Pestañas

2.9.- Cadera

2.10.- Espalda

3.1.- I

3.2.- K

3.3.- A

3.4.- J

3.5.- B

3.6.- G

3.7.- C

3.8.- E

3.9.- F

3.10.- D

4.1.- Neck

4.2.- Bladder

4.3.- Chest

4.4.- Tongue

4.5.- Lungs

4.6.- Waist

4.7.- Toes

4.8.- Wrist

4.9.- Nail

4.10.- Lips

5.1.- pies

5.2.- labios

5.3.- muñeca

5.4.- orejas

5.5.- cuello

5.6.- manos

5.7.- ojos

5.8.- dientes

5.9.- rodillas

5.10.- cabello

Translations:

1.- My wife has a beautiful and delicate **neck**.

2.- She gets green **eyes** if she gets angry.

3.- The **brain** has to exercise with reading.

4.- The man must have short and clean **nails**.

5.- The **chest** protects the **heart** and **lungs**.

6.- Drinking enough water helps to keep the **kidneys** healthy.

7.- Do not rest your **elbows** on the table, or speak with your **mouth** full.

8.- His **feet** seemed to not touch the floor.

9.- She caressed his **hair** with her **fingers**.

10.- He rubbed his **hands** waiting for his gift.

Story:

1. De por vida. – For life.

2. Nuevas historias. – New stories.

3. Grande, verde, y aterrador. – Big, green and scary.

4. En nuestros apartamentos. – In our apartments.

5. Un televisor. – A television.

6. En el robot. – In the robot.

Chapter 21

FOOD

When you travel to Spain or Latin America, and we hope it will be soon, we're sure that you will want to enjoy local food or at least be able to order a coffee. Don't worry because, in this chapter, you will find the vocabulary of the main foods in Spanish and other related words. As always, they come with didactic examples and exercises for you to practice your order. Enjoy your meal, or better said, ¡Buen provecho!

First, we will review the meals of the day (**breakfast, lunch, dinner**), remembering that they also function as verbs (to have breakfast / lunch / dinner).

- Desayuno - Breakfast
- Desayunar – To have breakfast
- Almuerzo - Lunch
- Almorzar - To have lunch
- Cena - Dinner
- Cenar – To have dinner
- Merienda - Snack
- Merendar - To snack
- Postre - Dessert

Examples:

1. - La cena será en mi casa.

   - Dinner will be at my house.

2. - Vamos a almorzar con mamá.

   - Let's have lunch with mom.

3. - El desayuno está servido.

- Breakfast is served.
4. - Hay helado de postre.
   - There is ice cream for dessert.

Now let's look at some essential foods:

- Grains / Granos:
  - Rice - Arroz
  - Corn - Maíz
  - Wheat - Trigo
  - Beans - Frijoles

- Meats / Carnes:
  - Beef - Res
  - Pork - Puerco
  - Fish - Pescado
  - Chicken - Pollo
  - Seafood - Mariscos

- Vegetables and legumes / vegetales y legumbres:
  - Tomato - Tomate
  - Onion - Cebolla
  - Garlic - Ajo
  - Banana - Plátano
  - Potato - Papa
  - Carrot - Zanahoria
  - Avocado - Aguacate
  - Lettuce - Lechuga
  - Cabbage - Repollo

- Fruits / Frutas:
  - Lemon - Limón
  - Orange - Naranja
  - Strawberry - Fresa
  - Cherry - Cereza
  - Apple - Manzana
  - Pear - Pera
  - Peach - Durazno
  - Grapes - Uvas

- Dairy products / Lácteos:
  - Milk - Leche
  - Butter - Mantequilla
  - Cheese - Queso
  - Yogurt - Yogurt

- Drinks / Bebidas:
  - Water - Agua
  - Juice - Jugo
  - Coffee - Café
  - Tea - Té
  - Wine - Vino
  - Beer - Cerveza
  - Soda - Soda

- Others / Otros:
  - Salt - Sal
  - Sugar – Azúcar

- Oil - Aceite
- Vinegar - Vinagre

- Other Food / Otras comidas:
  - Bread - Pan
  - Eggs - Huevos
  - Soup - Sopa
  - Salad - Ensalada

- Desserts and sweets / Postres y dulces:
  - Ice cream - Helado
  - Chocolate - Chocolate
  - Cake - Pastel
  - Jam - Mermelada
  - Cookie - Galleta

- Sausages / Embutidos:
  - Ham - Jamón
  - Bacon - Tocineta
  - Sausage - Salchicha
  - Chorizo - Chorizo

And of course, we need these things in order to eat:
  - Plate - Plato
  - Spoon - Cuchara
  - Knife - Cuchillo
  - Fork - Tenedor
  - Glass - Vaso
  - Cup - Taza

- Napkin - Servilleta

Examples:

1. - Los **tomates** están en la nevera.

   - The **tomatoes** are in the fridge.

2. - A José no le gusta el **pescado**.

   - José doesn't like **fish**.

3. - Al arroz le falta **sal**.

   - Rice lacks **salt**.

4. - Mi **jugo** de **naranja** sin **azúcar** por favor.

   - My **orange juice** without **sugar** please.

5. - A Daniela le gusta el **helado** de **chocolate**.

   - Daniela likes **chocolate ice cream**.

6. - Mesonero, me trae por favor una **servilleta**.

   - Waiter, please bring me a **napkin**.

———————————

Exercises:

1.- Write the following foods in Spanish.

     1.1.- Pork   _____

     1.2.- Avocado   _____

     1.3.- Beans   _____

     1.4.- Eggs   _____

     1.5.- Cheese   _____

     1.6.- Bread   _____

     1.7.- Coffee   _____

     1.8.- Juice   _____

     1.9.- Butter   _____

     1.10.- Chorizo   _____

2.- Select the food that belongs to the mentioned group.

     2.1.- Drinks

     a.- mantequilla

     b.- tocineta

     c.- cerveza

     2.2.- Grains

     a.- arroz

     b.- ajo

     c.- té

     2.3.- Meats

     a.- pan

     b.- res

c.- café

2.4.- Dairy

a.- queso

b.- limón

c.- azúcar

2.5.- Fruits

a.- pescado

b.- plato

c.- fresa

2.6.- Vegetable and legumes

a.- vino

b.- yogurt

c.- cebolla

2.7.- Sausages

a.- leche

b.- jamón

c.- tomate

2.8.- Desserts and sweets

a.- cerdo

b.- frijoles

c.- helado

2.9.- Meals

a.- sopa

b.- tenedor

c.- desayuno

2.10.- Fruits

a.- cerveza

b.- naranja

c.- cena

3.- Select the correct option.

3.1.- María likes coffee with...

a.- tomate.

b.- limón.

c.- leche.

3.2.- Hens lay...

a.- frijoles.

b.- huevos.

c.- cuchillos.

3.3.- I like butter on my...

a.- pan.

b.- chocolate.

c.- vino.

3.4.- I want a glass of...

a.- agua.

b.- maíz.

c.- pescado.

3.5.- She drinks red...

a.- leche.

b.- vino.

c.- helado.

3.6.- The salad has tomato and...

a.- chocolate.

b.- chorizo.

c.- lechuga.

3.7.- I want to eat fresh …. on the beach.

a.- vinagre

b.- pescado

c.- tenedor

3.8.- The first meal of the day is...

a.- la cena.

b.- el almuerzo.

c.- el desayuno.

3.9.- He needs a … of coffee.

a.- taza

b.- servilleta

c.- manzana

3.10.- You need a spoon for the...

a.- pan.

b.- sopa.

c.- cerveza.

4.- Write the following food-related words in English.

      4.1.- almuerzo   _____

      4.2.- sopa   _____

      4.3.- pollo   _____

      4.4.- arroz   _____

      4.5.- ensalada   _____

      4.6.- papas   _____

      4.7.- sal   _____

      4.8.- cerveza   _____

      4.9.- cuchara   _____

      4.10.- helado   _____

5.- Answer true (V = **Verdad**) or false (F = **Falso**).

      5.1.- The last meal of the day is: *desayuno*.

      F

      V

      5.2.- Soup is eaten with a: *cuchillo*.

      F

      V

      5.3.- *Pan* goes well with butter or jam.

      F

      V

      5.4.- *Pescado* comes from the sea.

      F

      V

5.5.- *Queso* is a dairy product.

F

V

5.6.- *Trigo* is a fruit.

F

V

5.7.- *Mariscos* is a sausage.

F

V

5.8.- *Res* is a very good dessert.

F

V

5.9.- We must have *desayuno* after 2pm.

F

V

5.10.- Strawberries, oranges and apples are *frutas*.

F

V

Translations:

Translate the following sentences into English:

1.- El **desayuno** es la comida más importante del día.

_____

2.- Mi madre preparaba las mejores **sopas** de **pollo**.

_____

3.- A Paola no le gustan los **tomates**.

_____

4.- Elizabeth toma el **café** muy caliente.

_____

5.- El **tenedor** a la izquierda, **cuchillo** y **cuchara** a la derecha.

_____

6.- Me gusta **desayunar pan** tostado con **huevos** y **tocineta**.

_____

7.- Es sano tomar **jugos** de **limón** y de **naranja**.

_____

8.- El mejor **helado** es el de **chocolate**.

_____

9.- No olvides tomar 8 **vasos** de **agua** al día.

_____

10.- **Vino** rojo con **res** y **cerdo**, **vino** blanco con **pollo** y **pescado**.

_____

Story:

Hay una famosa frase que dice "el cliente siempre tiene la razón". Pero se trata de algo **engañoso**. Por ejemplo, para una **niñera**, el cliente puede ser un par de niños de cinco años que muy probablemente no tienen la razón. Ese fue el caso de Andrea, la **niñera**, y Luis y Luisa, los hermanos **gemelos**. Los padres de los niños iban a estar fuera de la ciudad por un fin de semana, y Andrea tenía que quedarse con ellos y cuidarlos. Andrea necesitaba el dinero, pero en realidad no era la mejor de las niñeras. Así que, la primera noche, **desesperada** por distraer a los niños, los dejó ver cualquier película que quisieran en televisión. Así fue como los **gemelos** de cinco años, siendo demasiados **jóvenes** para eso, vieron una aterradora película sobre el fin del mundo, lo cual les dio demasiadas ideas locas.

El segundo día, los niños estaban asustados, y Andrea no pudo explicarles que el fin del mundo no iba a llegar ese día. Igualmente, tuvo que ayudarlos a **proteger** las **puertas** y **ventanas** de la casa. Y el dinero para **emergencias** que tenían lo gastaron todo en comida para el fin del mundo, incluyendo carnes y sopas en latas, mermeladas, y algunos dulces, porque incluso en el fin del mundo los niños van a querer comer galletas. Por supuesto, el mundo no se acabó ese día, pero cuando llegaron los padres, sí se acabó el **contrato** de Andrea.

Vocabulary:

1. Engañoso – Misleading
2. Niñera – Babysitter
3. Gemelos – Twins
4. Desesperada – Desperate
5. Jóvenes – Young
6. Proteger – Protect
7. Puertas – Doors
8. Ventanas – Windows
9. Emergencias – Emergencies
10. Contrato – Contract

Translated Story:

There is a famous phrase that says "the customer is always right". But this is **misleading**. For example, for a **babysitter**, the customers may be a couple of five-year-olds who are probably not right. That was the case with Andrea, the **babysitter**, and Luis and Luisa, the **twins**. The children's parents were going to be out of town for a weekend, and Andrea had to stay with them and take care of them. Andrea needed the money, but she really wasn't the best babysitter. So, the first night, **desperate** to distract the children, she let them watch whatever movie they wanted on television. That's how the five-year-old **twins**, being too **young** for that, watched a scary movie about the end of the world, which gave them too many crazy ideas.

On the second day, the children were scared, and Andrea could not explain to them that the end of the world was not going to come that day. Likewise, she had to help them **protect** the **doors** and **windows** of the house. And the **emergency** money they had they spent on food for the end of the world, including meats and soups in cans, jams, and some sweets, because even at the end of the world children are going to want to eat cookies. Of course, the world didn't end that day, but when the parents arrived, Andrea's **contract** did come to an end.

Questions:

1. ¿Quién siempre tiene la razón? _____

   Who is always right?

2. ¿Quién era la niñera? _____

   Who was the babysitter?

3. ¿Qué edad tienen los gemelos? _____

   How old are the twins?

4. ¿Qué vieron en televisión? _____

   What did they watch on television?

5. ¿Para qué era el dinero? _____

   What was the money for?

6. ¿Qué siempre quieren comer los niños? _____

   What do children always want to eat?

Answers:

1.1.- Cerdo

1.2.- Aguacate

1.3.- Frijoles

1.4.- Huevos

1.5.- Queso

1.6.- Pan

1.7.- Café

1.8.- Jugo

1.9.- Mantequilla

1.10.- Chorizo

2.1.- c

2.2.- a

2.3.- b

2.4.- a

2.5.- c

2.6.- c

2.7.- b

2.8.- c

2.9.- c

2.10.- b

3.1.- c

3.2.- b

3.3.- a

3.4.- a

3.5.- b

3.6.- c

3.7.- b

3.8.- c

3.9.- a

3.10.- b

4.1.- lunch

4.2.- soup

4.3.- chicken

4.4.- rice

4.5.- salad

4.6.- potatoes

4.7.- salt

4.8.- beer

4.9.- spoon

4.10.- ice cream

5.1.- F

5.2.- F

5.3.- V

5.4.- V

5.5.- V

5.6.- F

5.7.- F

5.8.- F

5.9.- F

5.10.- V

Translations:

1.- **Breakfast** is the most important meal of the day.

2. My mother made the best **chicken soups**.

3.- Paola doesn't like **tomatoes**.

4.- Elizabeth drinks very hot **coffee**.

5.- The **fork** on the left, **knife** and **spoon** on the right.

6. I like **breakfast** with toasted **bread** with **eggs** and **bacon**.

7. It is healthy to drink **lemon** and **orange juice**.

8.- The best **ice cream** is **chocolate**.

9.- Don't forget to drink 8 **glasses** of **water** a day.

10.- Red **wine** with **beef** and **pork**, white **wine** with **chicken** and **fish**.

Story:

1. El cliente. – The customer.

2. Andrea. – Andrea.

3. Cinco años. – Five years old.

4. Una película sobre el fin del mundo. – A film about the end of the world.

5. Para emergencias. – For emergencies.

6. Galletas. – Cookies.

Chapter 22

CLIMATE AND SEASONS

Congratulations! You have reached the final chapter of this book. It is a good time to review and revise the previous topics and realize just how much you have learned! Now all you have to do is travel to Spain or a Latin American country, and the only thing you have left to worry about is the clothes you are going to wear. That depends on the climate, the time of year, and the place you want to visit, so in this chapter, you will learn everything about the weather and the seasons. Grab your coat or sunscreen, and let's see what the weather's like.

First, we are going to review the seasons of the year in Spanish.

- Spring - Primavera
- Summer - Verano
- Autumn - Otoño
- Winter - Invierno

Examples:

1. - Las flores nacen en **primavera**.

   - The flowers are born in **spring**.

2. - Me gusta el **invierno** en España.

   - I like **winter** in Spain.

3. - Las hojas caen en **otoño**.

   - The leaves fall in **autumn**.

4. - Este **verano** iremos a la playa.

   - This **summer** we will go to the beach.

Now we are going learn some weather conditions in Spanish vocabulary.

- Hot - Calor
- Warm - Cálido
- Cold - Frío
- Sun - Sol
- Sunny - Soleado
- Cloud - Nube
- Cloudy - Nublado
- Wind - Viento
- Storm - Tormenta
- Rain - Lluvia
- Rainy - Lluvioso
- To rain - Llover
- Hurricane - Huracán
- Snow - Nieve

Examples:

1. - Hoy va a **llover**.

   - Today it's going to **rain**.

2. - Quiero ver la **nieve**.

   - I want to see the **snow**.

3. - Se acerca una **tormenta**.

   - A **storm** is coming.

4. - Ayer estuvo **nublado** todo el día.

   - Yesterday it was **cloudy** all day.

In Spanish, cold or warm weather is described using the conjunction **hace (makes)** of the verb **hacer (to make).** Another way uses the conjunction **está (is)** plus the verb **hacer (to make)** in gerund form: **haciendo (making)**.

Examples:

1. -It's hot:

    - **Hace** calor. / **Está haciendo** calor.

2. -It's cold:

    - **Hace** frío. / **Está haciendo** frío.

––––––––––––––––––

Exercises:

1.- Complete the sentence with the options in brackets.

    1.1.- In summer there is a lot of _____. (frio, nieve, calor)

    1.2.- Clouds produce _____. (sol, lluvia, primavera)

    1.3.- The _____ falls in winter. (nube, verano, nieve)

    1.4.- _____ is the season of flowers. (sol, frio, primavera)

    1.5.- The _____ shines this morning. (sol, huracán, otoño)

    1.6.- A strong _____ blows. (verano, nube, viento)

    1.7.- There are dark clouds. It's going to _____. (calor, invierno, llover)

    1.8.- Put on a coat, it's _____. (calor, soleado, frio)

    1.9.- The leaves change color in _____. lluvia, nieve, otoño)

    1.10.- The sun is covered by _____. (nieve, lluvia, nubes)

2.- Write the seasons and climates in Spanish.

    2.1.- Spring   _____

    2.2.- Storm   _____

    2.3.- Heat   _____

    2.4.- Cloud   _____

    2.5.- Autumn   _____

    2.6.- Snow   _____

    2.7.- Summer   _____

    2.8.- Sunny   _____

    2.9.- Rainy   _____

    2.10.- Hurricane   _____

3.- Link the seasons and climates with those located in the column on the right.

    3.1.- Snow   A.- Nublado

    3.2.- Wind   B.- Invierno

3.3. Cold	C.- Lluvia
3.4.- Winter	D.- Soleado
3.5.- Sun	E.- Otoño
3.6.- Cloudy	F.- Viento
3.7.- Rain	G.- Cálido
3.8.- Autumn	H.- Sol
3.9.- Warm	I.- Nieve
3.10.- Sunny	J.- Frío

4.- Write the following seasons and climates in English.

4.1.- Invierno _____

4.2.- Hace calor. _____

4.3.- Lluvia _____

4.4.- Nieve _____

4.5.- Primavera _____

4.6.- Está haciendo frío. _____

4.7.- Tormenta _____

4.8.- El día está soleado. _____

4.9.- Otoño _____

4.10.- Verano _____

5.- Select the correct option.

5.1.- The season of flowers.

a.- Primavera

b.- Nieve

c.- Verano

5.2.- The planet revolves around the _____.

a.- Huracán

b.- Otoño

c.- Sol

5.3.- It falls in winter when its coldest.

a.- Lluvia

b.- Nieve

c.- Nube

5.4.- The warmest season.

a.- Invierno

b.- Verano

c.- Otoño

5.5.- Rain falls from them:

a.- Flores

b.- Primavera

c.- Nubes

5.6.- The coldest season.

a.- Invierno

b.- Verano

c.- Primavera

5.7.- They are part of a storm.

a.- Sol y calor

b.- Lluvia y viento

c.- Frío y sol

5.8.- Leaves fall in which season?

a.- Otoño

b.- Primavera

C.- Nublado

5.9.- They are common in the summer.

a.- Nieve y lluvia

b.- Nubes y frío

c.- Sol y calor

5.10.-When it's sunny and with high temperatures,

a.- esta lluvioso.

b.- está haciendo frío.

c.- está haciendo calor.

Translations:

Translate the following sentences:

1.- En mi país hay dos **estaciones**, seca y **lluviosa**.

_____

2.- Enero es el mes más **frío** del año.

_____

3.- Yo prefiero el clima **frío** al **calor**.

_____

4.- Mi amiga se pone triste en los días **nublados**.

_____

5.- En **verano** vamos a la playa a disfrutar del mar, arena y **sol**.

_____

6.- A ella le gusta dormir con el sonido de la **lluvia**.

_____

7.- Fuimos a Madrid en **otoño**.

_____

8.- ¡Cuidado en la temporada de **huracanes**!

_____

9.- Parece que se acerca una **tormenta**.

_____

10.- Los pingüinos son felices en la **nieve**.

_____

Story:

Dicen que todas las historias tienen dos **lados**. Ambos **lados** pueden ser tan **dramáticos** como **entretenidos**. En mi familia, mi mamá y su hermana tienen ciertas diferencias. Mi mamá nunca aprobó el estilo de la vida de mi tía, y mi tía nunca le perdonó que no la apoyara. Esto no significa que sean **enemigas**. Simplemente significa que las cenas en familia cuando mi tía nos visita son particularmente divertidas. Mi mamá es una mujer muy seria y **organizada** que planeó toda su vida desde muy joven y fue muy **exitosa**. Mi tía es una mujer aventurera y, bueno, **honestamente** no sé mucho de ella, porque mi mamá dice que es una mala **influencia**.

Cuando mi tía nos cuenta sobre cómo sobrevivió un invierno en Finlandia, mi mamá me recuerda que fue algo muy **solitario**. Cuando mi tía nos cuenta sobre la vez que se perdió en México, mi mamá se molesta porque arriesgó su vida. Pero, **finalmente**, las hermanas tuvieron que hacer las paces. Porque ahora yo me uní a mi tía en sus viajes. Y cuando le cuento a mi mamá sobre todos los amigos que hice en Alemania, mi mamá está feliz de que mi tía y yo viajemos juntas.

Vocabulary:

1. Lados – Sides
2. Dramáticos – Dramatic
3. Entretenidos – Entertaining
4. Enemigas – Enemies
5. Organizada – Organized
6. Exitosa – Successful
7. Honestamente – Honestly
8. Influencia – Influence
9. Solitario – Lonely
10. Finalmente – Finally

Translated Story:

They say every story has two **sides**. Both **sides** can be as **dramatic** as they can be **entertaining**. In my family, my mom and her sister have certain differences. My mom never approved of my aunt's lifestyle, and my aunt never forgave her for not supporting her. This doesn't mean they are **enemies**. It simply means that dinners in the family when my aunt visits us are particularly fun. My mom is a very serious and **organized** woman that planned her entire life from being very young, and she was very **successful**. My aunt is an adventurous woman and, well, I **honestly** don't know much about her, because my mom says that she is a bad **influence**.

When my aunt tells us about how she survived a winter in Finland, my mom reminds me that it was something really **lonely**. When my aunt tells us about the time she got lost in Mexico, my mom gets upset because she risked her life. But, **finally**, the sisters had to make peace. Because now I joined my aunt in her trips. And when I tell my mom about all the friends I made in Germany, my mom is happy that my aunt and I travel together.

Questions:

1. ¿Cuántos lados tienen las historias? _____

   How many sides do stories have?

2. ¿Las hermanas son enemigas? _____

   Are the sisters enemies?

3. ¿Cómo es la mamá? _____

   What is the mom like?

4. ¿Quién es una mala influencia? _____

   Who is the bad influence?

5. ¿Dónde fue solitario? _____

   Where was lonely?

6. ¿Cómo está la mamá al final? _____

   How is the mom in the end?

Answers:

1.1.- calor

1.2.- lluvia

1.3.- nieve

1.4.- Primavera

1.5.- sol

1.6.- viento

1.7.- llover

1.8.- frío

1.9.- otoño

1.10.- nubes

2.1.- Primavera

2.2.- Tormenta

2.3.- Calor

2.4.- Nube

2.5.- Otoño

2.6.- Nieve

2.7.- Verano

2.8.- Soleado

2.9.- Lluvioso

2.10.- Huracán

3.1 .- I

3.2 .- F

3.3 .- J

3.4 .- B

3.5 .- H

3.6 .- A

3.7 .- C

3.8 .- E

3.9 .- G

3.10 .- D

4.1.- Winter

4.2.- It's hot.

4.3.- Rain

4.4.- Snow

4.5.- Spring

4.6.- It's cold.

4.7.- Storm

4.8.- The day is sunny.

4.9.- Autumn

4.10.- Summer

5.1 .- a

5.2 .- c

5.3 .- b

5.4 .- b

5.5 .- c

5.6 .- a

5.7 .- b

5.8 .- a

5.9 .- c

5.10 .- c

Translations:

1.- In my country there are two **seasons**, dry and **rainy**.

2.- January is the **coldest** month of the year.

3. I prefer **cold** over **hot** weather.

4.- My friend gets sad on **cloudy** days.

5.- In **summer** we go to the beach to enjoy the sea, sand, and **sun**.

6.- She likes to sleep with the sound of the **rain**.

7.- We went to Madrid in **autumn**.

8.- Be careful in the **hurricane** season!

9.- It seems that a **storm is coming**.

10.- Penguins are happy in the **snow**.

Story:

1. Dos. – Two.

2. No. – No.

3. Seria y organizada. – Serious and organized.

4. La tía. – The aunt.

5. En Finlandia. – In Finland.

6. Feliz. – Happy.

CONCLUSION

¡¡Felicitaciones!! You have come such a long way, which brings satisfaction and pride to those of us who have worked on this book's production. It should also be a source of pride and joy for you as you have started your command of the Spanish language off on the right foot. We sincerely hope that it has helped you, and above all, that you have enjoyed it. We trust that the process of reading, understanding, and practicing with the exercises and translations has fulfilled the primary goal of helping you understand, speak, and write in Spanish.

These books do not finish when the last page is read, but they stay with us for a long time in our memory and through how we use what we have learned. That is our humble aspiration: that this book accompanies you on your travels, in your interactions with Spanish-speaking people, and that it serves as a constant guide to the beginning of your command of the beautiful language of Cervantes, Neruda, and Gabriel García Márquez.

From this point, there is still a long way to go. We recommend that you use this book as support and consultation of the language, but you must also develop your knowledge and use of the Spanish language through other means. For example, our advice is to try and watch movies in Spanish without using subtitles. You may not understand much at first, but little by little, you will realize that progress in learning is constant and irreversible: you will no longer forget what you learn. Another recommended strategy is to listen to songs in Spanish. They are very beautiful, and the exercise will help you on your journey.

Try to read texts written in Spanish, either physically or online. Cultivate friendships with Spanish-speaking people through the internet. Meet and interact with Spanish speakers if you can, as this will help you improve your pronunciation of the language. If you are young, we suggest that an adult in your family checks those contacts. And of course, if it is within your means, plan your vacations to beautiful Spanish-speaking countries. Force yourself to talk and interact without translators or dictionaries. You will see how it is possible to do so, and you will soon be a bilingual expert.

Finally, we want to thank you for sharing this experience with us and, to say goodbye, we will do it in your new language:

¡Adiós!

Made in the USA
Middletown, DE
14 December 2022

18540103R00190